THE SHORTER POEMS OF
JOHN MILTON

THE POETRY BOOKSHELF

General Editor: James Reeves

Robert Graves: *English and Scottish Ballads*
Tom Scott: *Late Medieval Scots Poetry*
William Tydeman: *English Poetry 1400–1580*
Martin Seymour-Smith: *Shakespeare's Sonnets*
James Reeves: *John Donne*
Maurice Hussey: *Jonson and the Cavaliers*
Jack Dalglish: *Eight Metaphysical Poets*
James Reeves and Martin Seymour-Smith: *Andrew Marvell*
Dennis Burden: *John Milton*
V. de S. Pinto: *Poetry of the Restoration*
Roger Sharrock: *John Dryden*
James Reeves: *Jonathan Swift*
John Heath-Stubbs: *Alexander Pope*
Donald Davie: *The Late Augustans*
F. W. Bateson: *William Blake*
G. S. Fraser: *Robert Burns*
Roger Sharrock: *William Wordsworth*
James Reeves: *S. T. Coleridge*
Robin Skelton: *Lord Byron*
John Holloway: *P. B. Shelley*
James Reeves: *John Clare*
Robert Gittings: *John Keats*
Edmund Blunden: *Alfred Lord Tennyson*
James Reeves: *Robert Browning*
James Reeves: *Emily Dickinson*
James Reeves: *G. M. Hopkins*
David Wright: *Seven Victorian Poets*
James Reeves: *The Modern Poets' World*
James Reeves: *D. H. Lawrence*

JOHN MILTON

THE SHORTER POEMS OF
JOHN MILTON

Edited with an Introduction and Commentary

by
DENNIS H. BURDEN

HEINEMANN
LONDON

Heinemann Educational Books Ltd
LONDON MELBOURNE EDINBURGH
SINGAPORE JOHANNESBURG
TORONTO AUCKLAND
IBADAN HONG KONG
NAIROBI

SBN 435 15053 7

Published by
Heinemann Educational Books Ltd
48 Charles Street, London W1X 8AH
Printed in Great Britain by Morrison and Gibb Ltd
London and Edinburgh

CONTENTS

FOREWORD

THE first edition of Milton's shorter poems appeared in 1645 under the title *Poems of Mr John Milton, both English and Latin, Compos'd at several times*. A second edition appeared in 1673 under the title *Poems etc. upon Several Occasions, By Mr John Milton: both English and Latin, etc. Composed at several times*. This contained all the 1645 poems together with some poems written before 1645 but not included in the first edition, and other poems (chiefly sonnets) written between 1645 and 1673. Four sonnets in the latter group were not included in 1673 for political reasons. For details of these see the introductory note to the sonnets. The present edition includes all Milton's shorter poems in English except for some translations of various psalms. Poems which were printed in 1645 are marked [1645]. Poems first printed in 1673 are marked [1673]. The text and order of the poems (except the four sonnets mentioned above) is that of the 1673 edition with the original spelling and punctuation though obvious errors have been corrected.

SELECT BIBLIOGRAPHY

PROSE AND POETRY

The Student's Milton, ed. F. A. Patterson, New York, 1947.
The Poems of John Milton, ed. John Carey and Alastair Fowler, London, 1968.

BIOGRAPHY AND CRITICISM

Douglas Bush, *English Literature in the Earlier Seventeenth Century*, Oxford, 1945.
William Haller, *The Rise of Puritanism*, New York, 1938.
James Holly Hanford, *A Milton Handbook*, New York, 1947.
Samuel Johnson, 'Life of Milton', *Lives of the Poets*.
William Riley Parker, *Milton: a Biography*, Oxford, 1968.
F. T. Prince, *The Italian Element in Milton's Verse*, Oxford, 1954.
Rosemond Tuve, *Themes and Images in Five Poems by Milton*, Oxford, 1957.

CHRONOLOGY OF MILTON'S LIFE

1608   Born in London, son of a prosperous scrivener, who was generous in providing for the education of his son.

1620–5   Attended, after some private tuition at home, St Paul's Grammar School which provided a solid foundation of Christian doctrine and classical learning.

1625–32   At Christ's College, Cambridge. Milton found the syllabus at the university narrow and old-fashioned, but he had the opportunity for extensive reading of his own.

1632–8   Lived, through the support of his father, at Horton, Bucks, and devoted himself to private study in theology, philosophy and history. This intensive reading provided the learning which made him so massively intellectual a writer. Most of the poems in this volume were written in this period or in the last years of his residence at Cambridge. Milton's intention at this time was probably to go into the church, but, according to himself, his disapproval of episcopacy led him to abandon this.

1638–9   Travelled in Europe and became acquainted with Italian men of letters and culture. He returned to England on hearing of the outbreak of the Civil War.

1640–2   Lived in London. He married in 1642. It was in this period that he wrote his prose works arguing for the abolition of episcopacy and for the restoration of a simple apostolic system of church discipline.

1643–4   Engaged in writing on divorce, arguing for a considerable widening of the grounds upon which marriage could be dissolved. When Parliament took steps to bring the publication of books under strict control, Milton wrote *Areopagitica* in the defence of the freedom of the press.

1645–8   *Poems of Mr John Milton, both English and Latin*, published in 1645. This period saw Milton increasingly in opposition to the Presbyterian element in the Revolution and moving with the Independents whose strength was with Cromwell and the Army.

1649-59 Appointed Latin Secretary to the Council of State in 1649. During this period Milton was involved in extensive justification of the people's right through Parliament to arraign and execute Charles I. The country became increasingly disillusioned with the republican government, but Milton himself to the very end continued to write in support of a free commonwealth. He became blind early in the 1650's. His wife died in 1652, and he married again in 1656. His second wife died in 1658. Many of his sonnets were written during this and the preceding period.

1659-74 Arrested on the collapse of the Commonwealth but released after a short time. Considering his role as public apologist for Charles I's execution he was treated leniently at the restoration of Charles II. He lived the rest of his life in retirement in London, devoting himself to poetry. *Paradise Lost* was published in 1667 (second edition 1674), *Paradise Regained* and *Samson Agonistes* in 1671, and *Poems upon Several Occasions etc.* (a second edition, with some additions, of the 1645 volume) in 1673. He married again in 1663. He died in 1674. He was survived by his third wife and three daughters.

INTRODUCTION

I

WHEN Humphrey Moseley in his prefatory note to the 1645 edition says that 'the slightest Pamphlet is nowadayes more vendible then the Works of learnedest men', he gives no hint that the poet whom he is introducing was a most vehement and vigorous participant in religious and political controversy. What Moseley offers to his readers is a learned and courtly poet: the volume contained, besides the English poems, 87 pages of Latin poetry and 6 Italian sonnets. The title page also stresses the courtly aspect of some of the poems: 'The SONGS were set in Musick by Mr. HENRY LAWES Gentleman of the KINGS Chappel, and one of His MAIESTIES Private Musick'. In his preface Moseley goes on to say that the poems have been praised by 'the learnedst Academicks, both domestick and forrein', and his own linking of Milton with Spenser—accurate enough—puts Milton into line with the poetry of courtly aristocracy. Furthermore Milton himself had not shunned the aristocratic connection: he had collaborated with Lawes in *Arcades* and *Comus*. Nor is it just a selling point that Moseley is making, for when we come to read the poems we can see that the picture that the volume presents of Milton and his interests seems to be in some respects a very limited one. *Sonnet VIII*, 'Captain or Colonel, or Knight in Arms', would appear to indicate that Milton lived in the Civil War as a non-partisan poet whose only concern was with the non-party role of poetry. The picture of life that we get in *L'Allegro* and *Il Penseroso* is one of taste and elegance, far from partisan contentiousness. This does not of course hold with all the poems: the first poem in the volume, *On the*

Morning of Christs Nativity, and *Lycidas* present us with a Christian poet of some abrasiveness and power.

But if most of this poetry seems hardly to reflect Milton as he was in 1645 we must remember that most of it is comparatively early work, written more than a decade before. That Milton in 1645 rightly thought it good of its kind does not mean that it was in 1645 any more the sort of poetry that he wanted to write. But the publication of the volume was an important acknowledgement on Milton's part of his sense of his calling as a poet. His involvement in controversy did not mean that he had abandoned poetry. It is possibly that sense of being especially born to this art that prompts him in some of the poems in the volume to emphasize his precocity: he gives the date, 1630, when he had composed the *Nativity Ode*, adds a prefatory note to his translations of Psalms 114 and 136 that they 'were done by the Author at fifteen years old', and although the subject of *The Passion* turned out to be 'above the yeers he had', his publishing of it shows satisfaction with something in it. Nor, although the poems of 1645 were the first to be printed with his name, had Milton before that kept his talent hidden. *Comus* had been published by Henry Lawes in 1637, and Milton had contributed his poem 'On *Shakespear*' to the Second Folio, and *Lycidas* to the memorial volume to Edward King. *Arcades* and *Comus* had graced public occasions. There seems no reason to doubt Moseley's statement that 'The Authors more peculiar excellency in these studies, was too well known to conceal his Papers, or to keep me from attempting to sollicit them from him'. It is interesting that in *The Reason of Church-Government* (1642), the first of his prose writings to be published under his name, Milton had, in the Preface to the Second Book, made an emphatic declaration about his ambitions as a poet, and in particular recorded his determination to 'leave something so written to after-times, as they should not willingly let it die' and 'to fix all the industry and art I could unite to the adorning of my native tongue; not to make verbal curiosities the end, that were a toylsome vanity, but to be an interpreter & relater of the best and sagest things among mine own Citizens throughout this Iland in the mother dialect'. Milton, employed in his vocation of champion of conscience and spiritual liberty, ensures that his other vocation as poet is quite compatible with that and is made public. It must be admitted that the sort of poet that he outlines in *The Reason of Church-Government* seems much more compatible with the prose writer than the sort of poet that he appears to be in much of the 1645 volume. This springs from the fact that so many of these pieces were written so much earlier. Though none the less determined to fulfil his calling as a poet, the sort of poetry he wished to write naturally changed. In this edition it is the sonnets, and especially those written after 1645 and published in the 1673 edition, that have the gravity and intensity that seem to belong better to the role of serious Christian poet.

II

In his tractate *Of Education* (1644) Milton had written of poetry, comparing it with the disciplines of logic and rhetoric, that it is 'lesse suttle and fine, but more simple, sensuous and passionate'. This can justly be said of many of the poems in this volume, but Milton knew and was to come more fully to know that there was also a sort of poetry which was more logical and vehement. In *Paradise Lost*, for example, we find the intellectual and the poet working together, his moral energy, his intellectual passion, his love of art all collaborating in the writing. This more rigorous poetry is represented here—by the *Nativity Ode*, parts of *Lycidas* and some of the sonnets—but most of the poems in this volume are written with a mannered elegance and a charm appropriate to the form which he is using and the audience which is being addressed. It is worth stressing that most of these poems are not very personal and tell us very little about Milton himself. The title of the 1673 edition makes this very plain when it introduces them as *Poems etc. upon Several Occasions* since a great many of them are written to commemorate particular festivities or deaths or events in the Christian year. They are characteristically poems of a highly conscious art, an art concerned for the most part to beautify life and to sharpen our enjoyment of it. Sidney's well-known assertion of this principle in *An Apologie for Poetrie*:

> Nature never set forth the earth in so rich tapistry as divers poets have done, neither with so plesant rivers, fruitful trees, sweet-smelling flowers, nor whatsoever els may make the too much loved earth more lovely. Her world is brasen, the poets only deliver a golden.

provides the assumption about art by which so many of these poems are to be appreciated. It is a privilege not a deceit of art to provide a more beautiful world than that of the everyday. The poet in doing it becomes a creator and shows the dominance of the enlightened spirit of man. So poetry is a proper blend of nature and artifice.

Especially perhaps Milton's artifice shows itself in his awareness of writing within poetical traditions. The two important traditions of seventeenth-century poetry are both represented here. Firstly—and most important—there is the Spenserian, a mode of writing characterized by elaborate poeticalness of matter, style and diction. Some of the particularly distinguishing features of the last should be noticed: Milton's fondness for adjectives ending in 'y' for example, and for certain words which recur frequently: *tufted*, *warble*, *gloom*, etc. This sort of writing seemed much more creative to Milton than it does possibly to us. The creation of a deliberate poeticalness of effect is the reverse of stale. To be properly receptive to the style we have to acknowledge its creativeness, not merely in its selectiveness about words, but also in the way in which it creates new words or new applications for old ones. The persistent use of mythology is also a mode of poetical originality. Here Ovid, a poet of highly fanciful and lively invention, exerted an important influence on Milton. The other seventeenth-century tradition represented is that of Ben Jonson and his school, writers

4

who cultivated elegance and witty surprise. Particularly here we should notice Milton's love of paradox and of piquantly (sometimes harshly) changed metaphor.

But for all these obligations to tradition Milton creates in his best poems something uniquely his own. So many of the poems in this volume (*L'Allegro*, *Il Penseroso*, *Lycidas*, *Comus*, for example) seem to be the sort of poems that might have been written by any poet at this time since they use subjects and styles for which there was example and warrant. And yet there are no poems like them. A close study of them impresses us with their originality and variety and makes us understand the powerful influence which they had upon later English poetry.

THE STATIONER
TO THE READER.

It is not any private respect of gain, Gentle Reader, for the slightest Pamphlet is nowadayes more vendible then the Works of learnedest men; but it is the love I have to our own Language that hath made me diligent to collect, and set forth such Peeces both in Prose and Vers, as may renew the wonted honour and esteem of our English tongue: and it's the worth of these both English and Latin Poems, not the flourish of any prefixed encomions that can invite thee to buy them, though these are not without the highest Commendations and Applause of the learnedst Academicks, both domestick and forrein: And amongst those of our own Countrey, the unparallel'd attestation of that renowned Provost of Eaton, Sir Henry Wootton: I know not thy palat how it relishes such dainties, nor how harmonious thy soul is; perhaps more trivial Airs may please thee better. But howsoever thy opinion is spent upon these, that incouragement I have already received from the most ingenious men in their clear and courteous entertainment of Mr. Wallers late choice Peeces, hath once more made me adventure into the World, presenting it with these ever-green, and not to be blasted Laurels. The Authors more peculiar excellency in these studies, was too well known to conceal his Papers, or to keep me from attempting to sollicit them from him. Let the event guide it self which way it will, I shall deserve of the age, by bringing into the Light as true a Birth, as the Muses have brought forth since our famous Spencer wrote; whose Poems in these English ones are as rarely imitated, as sweetly excell'd. Reader, if thou art Eagle-eied to censure their worth, I am not fearful to expose them to thy exactest perusal.

Thine to command.

HUMPH. MOSELEY.

[*This preface to the 1645 edition was omitted in 1673.*]

ON THE MORNING OF Christs Nativity.

I.

This is the Month, and this the happy morn
Wherein the Son of Heav'ns eternal King,
Of wedded Maid, and Virgin Mother born,
Our great Redemption from above did bring;
For so the holy Sages once did sing,
   That he our deadly forfeit should release,
And with his Father work us a perpetual peace.

II.

That glorious Form, that Light unsufferable,
And that far-beaming blaze of Majesty,
Wherewith he wont at Heav'ns high Councel-Table,   10
To sit the midst of Trinal Unity,
He laid aside; and here with us to be,
   Forsook the Courts of everlasting Day,
And chose with us a darksom House of mortal Clay.

III.

Say Heav'nly Muse, shall not thy sacred vein
Afford a Present to the Infant God?
Hast thou no verse, no hymn, or solemn strein,
To welcome him to this his new abode,
Now while the Heav'n by the Suns team untrod,
   Hath took no print of the approching light,   20
And all the spangled host keep watch in squadrons bright?

Title] *1645 adds:* Compos'd 1629

8

See how from far upon the Eastern rode
The Star-led Wisards haste with odours sweet,
O run, prevent them with thy humble ode,
And lay it lowly at his blessed feet;
Have thou the honour first, thy Lord to greet,
 And joyn thy voice unto the Angel Quire,
From out his secret Altar toucht with hallowd fire.

The Hymn.

I.

IT was the Winter wilde,
While the Heav'n-born-childe,   30
 All meanly wrapt in the rude manger lies;
Nature in awe to him
Had doff't her gawdy trim,
 With her great Master so to sympathize:
It was no season then for her
To wanton with the Sun her lusty Paramour.

II.

Only with speeches fair
She woo's the gentle Air
 To hide her guilty front with innocent Snow,
And on her naked shame,   40
Pollute with sinfull blame,
 The Saintly Veil of Maiden white to throw,
Confounded, that her Makers eyes
Should look so neer upon her foul deformities.

III.

But he her fears to cease,
Sent down the meek-ey'd Peace,
   She crown'd with Olive green, came softly sliding
Down through the turning sphear
His ready Harbinger,
   With Turtle wing the amorous clouds dividing,   50
And waving wide her mirtle wand,
She strikes a universal Peace through Sea and Land.

IV.

No War, or Battels sound
Was heard the World around
   The idle Spear and Shield were high up hung;
The hooked Chariot stood
Unstain'd with hostile blood,
   The Trumpet spake not to the armed throng,
And Kings sate still with awfull eye,
As if they surely knew their sovran Lord was by.   60

V.

But peacefull was the night
Wherein the Prince of light
   His raign of peace upon the earth began:
The Winds with wonder whist
Smoothly the waters kist,
   Whispering new joyes to the milde Ocean,
Who now hath quite forgot to rave,
While Birds of Calm sit brooding on the charmed wave.

VI.

The Stars with deep amaze
Stand fixt in stedfast gaze,   70

Bending one way their pretious influence,
And will not take their flight,
For all the morning light,
    Or *Lucifer* that often warn'd them thence;
But in their glimmering Orbs did glow,
Untill their Lord himself bespake, and bid them go.

VII.

And though the shady gloom
Had given day her room,
    The Sun himself with-held his wonted speed,
And hid his head for shame,   80
As his inferiour flame,
    The new-enlightn'd world no more should need;
He saw a greater Sun appear
Then his bright Throne, or burning Axletree could bear.

VIII.

The Shepherds on the Lawn,
Or ere the point of dawn,
    Sate simply chatting in a rustick row;
Full little thought they than,
That the mighty *Pan*
    Was kindly come to live with them below;   90
Perhaps their loves, or else their sheep,
Was all that did their silly thoughts so busie keep.

IX.

When such musick sweet
Their hearts and ears did greet,
    As never was by mortall finger strook,
Divinely-warbl'd voice
Answering the stringed noise,
    As all their souls in blisfull rapture took:
The Air such pleasure loth to lose,
With thousand echo's still prolongs each heav'nly close.   100

X.

Nature that heard such sound
Beneath the hollow round
  Of *Cynthia*'s seat, the Airy region thrilling,
Now was almost won
To think her part was done,
  And that her reign had here its last fulfilling;
She knew such harmony alone
Could hold all Heav'n and Earth in happier union.

XI.

At last surrounds their sight
A Globe of circular light,   110
  That with long beams the shame-fac't night array'd,
The helmed Cherubim
And sworded Seraphim,
  Are seen in glittering ranks with wings displaid,
Harping in loud and solemn quire,
With unexpressive notes to Heav'ns new-born Heir.

XII.

Such Musick (as 'tis said)
Before was never made,
  But when of old the sons of morning sung,
While the Creator great   120
His Constellations set,
  And the well-ballanc't world on hinges hung,
And cast the dark foundations deep,
And bid the weltring waves their oozy channel keep.

XIII.

Ring out ye Crystall sphears,
Once bless our humane ears,
  (If ye have power to touch our senses so)

And let your silver chime
Move in melodious time;
   And let the Base of Heav'ns deep Organ blow,   130
And with your ninefold harmony
Make up full consort to th'Angelike symphony.

XIV.

For if such holy Song
Enwrap our fancy long,
   Time will run back, and fetch the age of gold,
And speckl'd vanity
Will sicken soon and die,
   And leprous sin will melt from earthly mould,
And Hell it self will pass away,
And leave her dolorous mansions to the peering day.   140

XV.

Yea Truth, and Justice then
Will down return to men,
   Orb'd in a Rain-bow; and like glories wearing
Mercy will sit between,
Thron'd in Celestial sheen,
   With radiant feet the tissued clouds down stearing,
And Heav'n as at some Festivall,
Will open wide the Gates of her high Palace Hall.

XVI.

But wisest Fate sayes no,
This must not yet be so,   150
   The Babe lies yet in smiling Infancy,
That on the bitter cross
Must redeem our loss;
   So both himself and us to glorifie:
Yet first to those ychain'd in sleep,
The wakeful trump of doom must thunder through the deep.

143–4 or'b . . . between,] Th'enameld *Arras* of the Rainbow wearing,
And Mercy set between, *1645*.

With such a horrid clang
As on mount *Sinai* rang
    While the red fire, and smouldring clouds out brake:
The aged Earth agast   160
With terrour of that blast,
    Shall from the surface to the center shake;
When at the worlds last session,
The dreadful Judge in middle Air shall spread his throne.

XVIII.

And then at last our bliss
Full and perfet is,
    But now begins; for from this happy day
Th'old Dragon under ground
In straiter limits bound,
    Not half so far casts his usurped sway,   170
And wroth to see his Kingdom fail,
Swindges the scaly Horrour of his foulded tail.

XIX.

The Oracles are dum,
No voice or hideous humm
    Runs through the arched roof in words deceiving.
Apollo from his shrine
Can no more divine,
    With hollow shreik the steep of *Delphos* leaving.
No nightly trance, or breathed spell,
Inspire's the pale-ey'd Priest from the prophetic cell.   180

XX.

The lonely mountains o're,
And the resounding shore,
    A voice of weeping heard, and loud lament;
From haunted spring, and dale
Edg'd with poplar pale,

The parting Genius is with sighing sent,
With flowre-inwov'n tresses torn
The Nimphs in twilight shade of tangled thickets mourn.

In consecrated Earth,
And on the holy Hearth,   190
   The *Lars*, and *Lemures* moan with midnight plaint,
In Urns, and Altars round,
A drear and dying sound
   Affrights the *Flamins* at their service quaint;
And the chill Marble seems to sweat,
While each peculiar power forgoes his wonted seat.

Peor, and *Baalim*,
Forsake their Temples dim,
   With that twice batter'd god of *Palestine*,
And mooned *Ashtaroth*,   200
Heav'ns Queen and Mother both,
   Now sits not girt with Tapers holy shine,
The Libyc *Hammon* shrinks his horn,
In vain the *Tyrian* Maids their wounded *Thamuz* mourn.

And sullen *Moloch* fled,
Hath left in shadows dred,
   His burning Idol all of blackest hue;
In vain with Cymbals ring,
They call the grisly King,
   In dismal dance about the furnace blue;   210
The brutish gods of *Nile* as fast,
Isis and *Orus*, and the Dog *Anubis* hast.

XXIV.

Nor is *Osiris* seen
In *Memphian* Grove, or Green,
   Trampling the unshowr'd Grass with lowings loud:
Nor can he be at rest
Within his sacred chest,
   Naught but profoundest Hell can be his shroud,
In vain with Timbrel'd Anthems dark
The sable-stoled Sorcerers bear his worshipt Ark.   220

XXV.

He feels from *Juda*'s Land
The dredded Infants hand,
   The rayes of *Bethlehem* blind his dusky eyn;
Nor all the Gods beside,
Longer dare abide,
   Not *Typhon* huge ending in snaky twine:
Our Babe to shew his Godhead true,
Can in his swadling bands controul the damned crew.

XXVI.

So when the Sun in bed,
Curtain'd with cloudy red,   230
   Pillows his chin upon an Orient wave,
The flocking shadows pale,
Troop to th'infernal Jail,
   Each fetter'd Ghost slips to his several grave,
And the yellow-skirted *Fayes*,
Fly after the Night-steeds, leaving their Moon-lov'd maze.

XXVII.

But see the Virgin blest,
Hath laid her Babe to rest.
   Time is our tedious Song should here have ending:
Heav'ns youngest teemed Star,   240
Hath fixt her polisht Car.

Her sleeping Lord with Handmaid Lamp attending:
And all about the Courtly Stable,
Bright-harnest Angels sit in order serviceable.

A Paraphrase on *Psalm* 114.

This and the following *Psalm* were done by the Author at fifteen years old.

[The *Paraphrase on Psalm 114* is omitted from this edition.]

Psalm 136.

LET us with a gladsom mind
Praise the Lord, for he is kind
 For his mercies ay endure,
 Ever faithfull, ever sure.

Let us blaze his Name abroad,
For of gods he is the God;
 For his, *&c.*

O let us his praises tell,
Who doth the wrathfull tyrants quell.   10
 For his, *&c.*

Who with his miracles doth make
Amazed Heav'n and Earth to shake.
 For his, *&c.*

Who by his wisdom did create
The painted Heav'ns so full of state.
 For his, *&c.*   20

Who did the solid Earth ordain
To rise above the watry plain.
   For his, &c.

Who by his all-commanding might,
Did fill the new-made world with light.
   For his, &c.

And caus'd the Golden-tressed Sun,
All the day long his cours to run.   30
   For his, &c.

The horned Moon to shine by night,
Amongst her spangl'd sisters bright.
   For his, &c.

He with his thunder-clasping hand,
Smote the first-born of *Egypt* Land.
   For his, &c.   40

And in despight of *Pharao* fell,
He brought from thence his *Israel*.
   For his, &c.

The ruddy waves he cleft in twain,
Of the *Erythræan* main.
   For his, &c.

The flouds stood still like Walls of Glass,
While the Hebrew Bands did pass.   50
   For his, &c.

But full soon they did devour
The Tawny King with all his power.
   For his, &c.

His chosen people he did bless
In the wastfull Wilderness.
   For his, *&c.*   60

In bloudy battel he brought down
Kings of prowess and renown.
   For his, *&c.*

He foild bold *Seon* and his host,
That rul'd the *Amorrean* coast.
   For his, *&c.*

And large-limb'd *Og* he did subdue,
With all his over-hardy crew.   70
   For his, *&c.*

And to his servant *Israel*,
He gave their Land therein to dwell.
   For his, *&c.*

He hath with a piteous eye
Beheld us in our misery.
   For his, *&c.*   80

And freed us from the slavery
Of the invading enemy.
   For his, *&c.*

All living creatures he doth feed,
And with full hand supplies their need.
   For his, *&c.*

Let us therfore warble forth
His mighty Majesty and worth.   90
   For his, *&c.*

That his mansion hath on high
Above the reach of mortal eye.
For his mercies ay endure,
Ever faithfull, ever sure.

[1645]

Anno aetatis 17.

On the Death of a fair Infant dying of a Cough.

I.

O FAIREST flower no sooner blown but blasted,
Soft silken Primrose fading timeslesslie,
Summers chief honour if thou hadst out-lasted,
Bleak winters force that made thy blossome drie;
For he being amorous on that lovely die
    That did thy cheek envermeil, thought to kiss
But kill'd alas, and then bewayl'd his fatal bliss.

II.

For since grim Aquilo his charioter
By boistrous rape th' Athenian damsel got,
He thought it toucht his Deitie full neer,   10
If likewise he some fair one wedded not,
Thereby to wipe away th' infamous blot,
    Of long-uncoupled bed, and childless eld,
Which 'mongst the wanton gods a foul reproach was held.

III.

So mounting up in ycie-pearled carr,
Through middle empire of the freezing aire
He wanderd long, till thee he spy'd from farr,

20

There ended was his quest, there ceast his care.
Down he descended from his Snow-soft chaire,
   But all unwares with his cold-kind embrace   20
Unhous'd thy Virgin Soul from her fair biding place.

IV.

Yet art thou not inglorious in thy fate;
For so *Apollo*, with unweeting hand
Whilome did slay his dearly-loved mate
Young *Hyacinth* born on *Eurota's* strand
Young *Hyacinth* the pride of *Spartan* land;
   But then transform'd him to a purple flower
Alack that so to change thee winter had no power.

V.

Yet can I not perswade me thou art dead
Or that thy coarse corrupts in earths dark wombe,   30
Or that thy beauties lie in wormie bed,
Hid from the world in a low delved tombe;
Could Heav'n for pittie thee so strictly doom?
   Oh no! for something in thy face did shine
Above mortalitie that shew'd thou wast divine.

VI.

Resolve me then oh Soul most surely blest
(If so it be that thou these plaints dost hear)
Tell me bright Spirit where e're thou hoverest
Whether above that high first-moving Spheare
Or in the Elisian fields (if such there were.)   40
   Oh say me true if thou wert mortal wight
And why from us so quickly thou didst take thy flight.

VII.

Wert thou some Starr which from the ruin'd roofe
Of shak't Olympus by mischance didst fall;
Which carefull *Jove* in natures true behoofe

Took up, and in fit place did reinstall?
Or did of late earths Sonnes besiege the wall
   Of sheenie Heav'n, and thou some goddess fled
Amongst us here below to hide thy nectar'd head?

VIII.

Or wert thou that just Maid who once before   50
Forsook the hated earth, O tell me sooth
And cam'st again to visit us once more?
Or wert thou that sweet smiling Youth?
Or that crown'd Matron sage white-robed truth?
   Or any other of that heav'nly brood
Let down in clowdie throne to do the world some good.

IX.

Or wert thou of the golden-winged hoast,
Who having clad thy self in humane weed,
To earth from thy præfixed seat didst poast,
And after short abode flie back with speed,   60
As if to shew what creatures Heav'n doth breed,
   Thereby to set the hearts of men on fire
To scorn the sordid world, and unto Heav'n aspire.

X.

But oh why didst thou not stay here below
To bless us with thy heav'n-lov'd innocence,
To slake his wrath whom sin hath made our foe
To turn Swift-rushing black perdition hence,
Or drive away the slaughtering pestilence,
   To stand 'twixt us and our deserved smart
But thou canst best perform that office where thou art.   70

XI.

Then thou the mother of so sweet a child
Her false imagin'd loss cease to lament,
And wisely learn to curb thy sorrows wild;

Think what a present thou to God hast sent,
And render him with patience what he lent;
   This if thou do he will an off-spring give,
That till the worlds last-end shall make thy name to live.

Anno Ætatis 19. *At a Vacation Exercise in the Colledge,
part* Latin, *part* English. *The* Latin *speeches ended,
the* English *thus began.*

Hail native Language, that by sinews weak
Didst move my first endeavouring tongue to speak,
And mad'st imperfect words with childish tripps,
Half unpronounc't, slide through my infant-lipps,
Driving dum silence from the portal dore,
Where he had mutely sate two years before:
Here I salute thee and thy pardon ask,
That now I use thee in my latter task:
Small loss it is that thence can come unto thee,
I know my tongue but little Grace can do thee: 10
Thou needst not be ambitious to be first,
Believe me I have thither packt the worst:
And, if it happen as I did forecast,
The daintest dishes shall be serv'd up last.
I pray thee then deny me not thy aide
For this same small neglect that I have made:
But haste thee strait to do me once a Pleasure,
And from thy wardrope bring thy chiefest treasure;
Not those new fangled toys, and triming slight
Which takes our late fantasticks with delight,   20
But cull those richest Robes, and gay'st attire

Which deepest Spirits, and choicest Wits desire:
I have some naked thoughts that rove about
And loudly knock to have their passage out;
And wearie of their place do only stay
Till thou hast deck't them in thy best aray;
That so they may without suspect or fears
Fly swiftly to this fair Assembly's ears;
Yet I had rather, if I were to chuse,
Thy service in some graver subject use,   30
Such as may make thee search thy coffers round,
Before thou cloath my fancy in fit sound:
Such where the deep transported mind may soare
Above the wheeling poles, and at Heav'ns dore
Look in, and see each blissful Deitie
How he before the thunderous throne doth lie,
Listening to what unshorn *Apollo* sings
To th' touch of golden wires, while *Hebe* brings
Immortal Nectar to her Kingly Sire:
Then passing through the Spherse of watchful fire,   40
And mistie Regions of wide air next under,
And hills of Snow and lofts of piled Thunder,
May tell at length how green-ey'd *Neptune* raves,
In Heav'ns defiance mustering all his waves;
Then sing of secret things that came to pass
When Beldam Nature in her cradle was;
And last of Kings and Queens and *Hero's* old,
Such as the wise *Demodocus* once told
In solemn Songs at King *Alcinous* feast,
While sad *Ulisses* soul and all the rest   50
Are held with his melodious harmonie
In willing chains and sweet captivitie.
But fie my wandring Muse how thou dost stray!
Expectance calls thee now another way,
Thou know'st it must be now thy only bent
To keep in compass of thy Predicament:

Then quick about thy purpos'd business come,
That to the next I may resign my Roome.

Then Ens *is represented as Father of the Prædicaments his ten Sons, whereof the Eldest stood for* Substance *with his Canons, which* Ens *thus speaking, explains.*

Good luck befriend thee Son; for at thy birth
The Faiery Ladies daunc't upon the hearth;   60
Thy drowsie Nurse hath sworn she did them spie
Come tripping to the Room where thou didst lie;
And sweetly singing round about thy Bed
Strew all their blessings on thy sleeping Head.
She heard them give thee this, that thou should'st still
From eyes of mortals walk invisible,
Yet there is something that doth force my fear,
For once it was my dismal hap to hear
A *Sybil* old, bow-bent with crooked age,
That far events full wisely could presage,   70
And in Times long and dark Prospective Glass
Fore-saw what future dayes should bring to pass,
Your Son, said she, (nor can you it prevent)
Shall subject be to many an Accident.
O're all his Brethren he shall Reign as King,
Yet every one shall make him underling,
And those that cannot live from him asunder
Ungratefully shall strive to keep him under,
In worth and excellence he shall out-go them,
Yet being above them, he shall be below them;   80
From others he shall stand in need of nothing,
Yet on his Brothers shall depend for Cloathing.
To find a Foe it shall not be his hap,
And peace shall lull him in her flowry lap;
Yet shall he live in strife, and at his dore
Devouring war shall never cease to roare:

25

Yea it shall be his natural property
To harbour those that are at enmity.
What power, what force, what mighty spell, if not
Your learned hands, can loose this Gordian knot?   90

The next Quantity *and* Quality, *spake in Prose, then* Relation *was call'd by his Name.*

Rivers arise; whether thou be the Son,
Of utmost *Tweed*, or *Oose*, or gulphie *Dun*,
Or *Trent*, who like some earth-born Giant spreads
His thirty Armes along the indented Meads,
Or sullen *Mole* that runneth underneath,
Or *Severn* swift, guilty of Maidens death,
Or Rockie *Avon*, or of Sedgie *Lee*,
Or Coaly *Tine*, or antient hallowed *Dee*,
Or *Humber* loud that keeps the *Scythians* Name,
Or *Medway* smooth, or Royal Towred *Thame*.   100

The rest was Prose.

[1673]

The Passion.

I.

ERE-while of Musick, and Ethereal mirth,
Wherewith the stage of Ayr and Earth did ring,
And joyous news of heav'nly Infants birth,
My muse with Angels did divide to sing;
But headlong joy is ever on the wing,
   In Wintry solstice like the shortn'd light
Soon swallow'd up in dark and long out-living night.

II.

For now to sorrow must I tune my song,
And set my Harp to notes of saddest wo,
Which on our dearest Lord did sease er'e long,   10

26

Dangers, and snares, and wrongs, and worse then so,
Which he for us did freely undergo.
    Most perfect *Heroe*, try'd in heaviest plight
Of labours huge and hard, too hard for human wight.

III.

He sov'ran Priest stooping his regal head
That dropt with odorous oil down his fair eyes,
Poor fleshly Tabernacle entered,
His starry front low-rooft beneath the skies;
O what a mask was there, what a disguise!
    Yet more; the stroke of death he must abide,   20
Then lies him meekly down fast by his Brethrens side.

IV.

These latest scenes confine my roving vers,
To this Horizon is my *Phœbus* bound,
His Godlike acts; and his temptations fierce,
And former sufferings other where are found;
Loud o're the rest *Cremona*'s Trump doth sound;
    Me softer airs befit, and softer strings
Of Lute, or Viol still, more apt for mournful things.

V.

Befriend me night best Patroness of grief,
Over the Pole thy thickest mantle throw,   30
And work my flatter'd fancy to belief,
That Heav'n and Earth are colour'd with my wo;
My sorrows are too dark for day to know:
    The leaves should all be black wheron I write,
And letters where my tears have washt a wannish white.

VI.

See see the Chariot, and those rushing wheels,
That whirl'd the Prophet up at *Chebar* flood,
My spirit som transporting *Cherub* feels,

To bear me where the Towers of *Salem* stood,
Once glorious Towers, now sunk in guiltless blood; 40
   There doth my soul in holy vision sit
In pensive trance, and anguish, and ecstatick fit.

VII.

Mine eye hath found that sad Sepulchral rock
That was the Casket of Heav'ns richest store,
And here though grief my feeble hands up lock,
Yet on the softned Quarry would I score
My plaining vers as lively as before;
   For sure so well instructed are my tears,
That they would fitly fall in order'd Characters.

VIII.

Or should I thence hurried on viewles wing, 50
Take up a weeping on the Mountains wilde,
The gentle neighbourhood of grove and spring
Would soon unbosom all thir Echoes milde,
And I (for grief is easily beguild)
   Might think th'infection of my sorrows loud,
Had got a race of mourners on som pregnant cloud.
*This Subject the Author finding to be above the yeers he had, when he wrote it,
   and nothing satisfi'd with what was begun, left it unfinisht.*
[1645]

On Time.

FLY envious *Time*, till thou run out thy race,
Call on the lazy leaden-stepping hours,
Whose speed is but the heavy Plummets pace;
And glut thy self with what thy womb devours,

Which is no more then what is false and vain,
And meerly mortal dross;
So little is our loss,
So little is thy gain.
For when as each thing bad thou hast entomb'd,
And last of all thy greedy self consum'd,   10
Then long Eternity shall greet our bliss
With an individual kiss;
And Joy shall overtake us as a flood,
When every thing that is sincerely good
And perfectly divine,
With Truth, and Peace, and Love shall ever shine
About the supreme Throne
Of him, t'whose happy-making sight alone,
When once our heav'nly-guided soul shall clime,
Then all this Earthy grosness quit,   20
Attir'd with Stars, we shall for ever sit,
    Triumphing over Death, and Chance, and thee O Time.

[1645]

Upon the Circumcision.

YE flaming Powers, and winged Warriours bright,
That erst with Musick, and triumphant song
First heard by happy watchful Shepherds ear,
So sweetly sung your Joy the Clouds along
Through the soft silence of the list'ning night;
Now mourn, and if sad share with us to bear
Your fiery essence can distill no tear,
Burn in your sighs, and borrow
Seas wept from our deep sorrow,
He who with all Heav'ns heraldry whilear   10

29

Enter'd the world, now bleeds to give us ease;
Alas, how soon our sin
   Sore doth begin
      His Infancy to sease!
O more exceeding love or law more just?
Just law indeed, but more exceeding love!
For we by rightful doom remediles
Were lost in death, till he that dwelt above
High thron'd in secret bliss, for us frail dust
Emptied his glory, ev'n to nakednes;   20
And that great Cov'nant which we still transgress
   Intirely satisfi'd,
   And the full wrath beside
Of vengeful Justice bore for our excess,
And seals obedience first with wounding smart
   This day, but O ere long
   Huge pangs and strong
      Will pierce more neer his heart.

[1645]

At a Solemn Musick.

BLEST pair of *Sirens*, pledges of Heav'ns joy,
Sphear-born harmonious Sisters, Voice, and Vers,
Wed your divine sounds, and mixt power employ
Dead things with inbreath'd sense able to pierce,
And to our high-rais'd phantasie present,
That undisturbed Song of pure concent,
Ay sung before the saphire-colour'd throne
To him that sits theron
With Saintly shout, and solemn Jubily,
Where the bright Seraphim in burning row   10
Their loud up-lifted Angel trumpets blow,

And the Cherubick host in thousand quires
Touch their immortal Harps of golden wires,
With those just Spirits that wear victorious Palms,
Hymns devout and holy Psalms
Singing everlastingly;
That we on Earth with undiscording voice
May rightly answer that melodious noise;
As once we did, till disproportion'd sin
Jarr'd against natures chime, and with harsh din   20
Broke the fair musick that all creatures made
To their great Lord, whose love their motion sway'd
In perfect Diapason, whilst they stood
In first obedience, and their state of good.
O may we soon again renew that Song,
And keep in tune with Heav'n, till God ere long
To his celestial consort us unite,
To live with him, and sing in endles morn of light.

[1645]

An Epitaph on the Marchioness of *Winchester*.

THIS rich Marble doth enterr
The honour'd Wife of *Winchester*,
A Vicounts daughter, an Earls heir,
Besides what her vertues fair
Added to her noble birth,
More then she could own from Earth.
Summers three times eight save one
She had told, alas too soon,
After so short time of breath,
To house with darkness, and with death.   10
Yet had the number of her days
Bin as compleat as was her praise,

31

Nature and fate had had no strife
In giving limit to her life.
Her high birth, and her graces sweet,
Quickly found a lover meet;
The Virgin quire for her request
The God that sits at marriage feast;
He at their invoking came
But with a scarce-wel-lighted flame;   20
And in his Garland as he stood,
Ye might discern a Cypress bud.
Once had the early Matrons run
To greet her of a lovely son,
And now with second hope she goes,
And calls *Lucina* to her throws;
But whether by mischance or blame
Atropos for *Lucina* came;
And with remorsles cruelty,
Spoil'd at once both fruit and tree: 30
The haples Babe before his birth
Had burial, yet not laid in earth,
And the languisht Mothers Womb
Was not long a living Tomb.
So have I seen som tender slip
Sav'd with care from Winters nip,
The pride of her carnation train,
Pluck't up by som unheedy swain,
Who onely thought to crop the flowr
New shot up from vernal showr;   40
But the fair blossom hangs the head
Side-ways as on a dying bed,
And those Pearls of dew she wears,
Prove to be presaging tears
Which the sad morn had let fall
On her hast-ning funerall.
Gentle Lady may thy grave

Peace and quiet ever have;
After this thy travel sore
Sweet rest sease thee evermore,   50
That to give the world encrease,
Shortned hast thy own lives lease;
Here, besides the sorrowing
That thy noble House doth bring,
Here be tears of perfect moan
Weept for thee in *Helicon*,
And some Flowers, and some Bays,
For thy Hears to strew the ways,
Sent thee from the banks of *Came*,
Devoted to thy vertuous name;   60
Whilst thou bright Saint high sit'st in glory.
Next her much like to thee in story,
That fair *Syrian* Shepherdess,
Who after yeers of barrenness,
The highly favour'd *Joseph* bore
To him that serv'd for her before,
And at her next birth much like thee,
Through pangs fled to felicity,
Far within the boosom bright
Of blazing Majesty and Light,   70
There with thee, new welcom Saint,
Like fortunes may her soul acquaint,
With thee there clad in radiant sheen,
No Marchioness, but now a Queen.

[1645]

SONG

On May *Morning.*

Now the bright morning Star, Dayes harbinger,
Comes dancing from the East, and leads with her
The Flowry *May*, who from her green lap throws
The yellow Cowslip, and the pale Primrose.
   Hail bounteous *May* that dost inspire
   Mirth and youth and warm desire,
   Woods and Groves are of thy dressing,
   Hill and Dale doth boast thy blessing.
Thus we salute thee with our early Song,
And welcom thee, and wish thee long.   10

[1645]

On Shakespear. 1630.

What needs my *Shakespear* for his honour'd Bones,
The labour of an age in piled Stones,
Or that his hallow'd reliques should be hid
Under a Star-ypointing *Pyramid?*
Dear son of memory, great heir of Fame,
What need'st thou such weak witness of thy name?
Thou in our wonder and astonishment
Hast built thy self a live-long Monument.
For whilst to th' shame of slow-endeavouring art,
Thy easie numbers flow, and that each heart   10
Hath from the leaves of thy unvalu'd Book,
Those Delphick lines with deep impression took,

34

Then thou our fancy of it self bereaving,
Dost make us Marble with too much conceaving;
And so Sepulcher'd in such pomp dost lie,
That Kings for such a Tomb would wish to die.

[1645]

On the University Carrier who sickn'd in the time of his vacancy, being forbid to go to London, by reason of the Plague.

HERE lies old *Hobson*, Death hath broke his girt,
And here alas, hath laid him in the dirt,
Or else the ways being foul, twenty to one,
He's here stuck in a slough, and overthrown.
'Twas such a shifter, that if truth were known,
Death was half glad when he had got him down;
For he had any time this ten yeers full,
Dodg'd with him, betwixt *Cambridge* and the Bull.
And surely, Death could never have prevail'd,
Had not his weekly course of carriage fail'd;   10
But lately finding him so long at home,
And thinking now his journeys end was come,
And that he had tane up his latest Inne,
In the kind office of a Chamberlin
Shew'd him his room where he must lodge that night,
Pull'd off his Boots, and took away the light:
If any ask for him, it shall be sed,
Hobson has supt, and's newly gon to bed.

[1645]

Another on the same.

HERE lieth one who did most truly prove,
That he could never die while he could move,
So hung his destiny never to rot
While he might still jogg on and keep his trot,
Made of sphear-metal, never to decay
Untill his revolution was at stay.
Time numbers motion, yet (without a crime
'Gainst old truth) motion number'd out his time:
And like an Engin mov'd with wheel and waight,
His principles being ceast, he ended strait,   10
Rest that gives all men life, gave him his death,
And too much breathing put him out of breath;
Nor were it contradiction to affirm
Too long vacation hastned on his term.
Meerly to drive the time away he sickn'd,
Fainted, and died, nor would with Ale be quickn'd;
Nay, quoth he, on his swooning bed out-stretched,
If I may not carry, sure I'le ne're be fetch'd,
But vow though the cross Doctors all stood hearers,
For one Carrier put down to make six bearers.   20
Ease was his chief disease, and to judge right,
He di'd for heaviness that his Cart went light,
His leasure told him that his time was com,
And lack of load, made his life burdensom,
That even to his last breath (ther be that say't)
As he were prest to death, he cry'd more waight;
But had his doings lasted as they were,
He had bin an immortal Carrier.
Obedient to the Moon he spent his date
In cours reciprocal, and had his fate   30

Linkt to the mutual flowing of the Seas,
Yet (strange to think) his wain was his increase:
His Letters are deliver'd all and gon,
Onely remains this superscription.

[1645]

L'Allegro.

HENCE loathed Melancholy
   Of *Cerberus*, and blackest midnight born,
In *Stygian* Cave forlorn.
   'Mongst horrid shapes, and shreiks, and sights unholy,
Find out some uncouth cell,
   Where brooding darknes spreads his jealous wings,
And the night-Raven sings;
   There under *Ebon* shades, and low-brow'd Rocks,
As ragged as thy Locks,
   In dark *Cimmerian* desert ever dwell.   10
But com thou Goddes fair and free,
In Heav'n ycleap'd *Euphrosyne*,
And by men, heart-easing Mirth,
Whom lovely *Venus* at a birth
With two sister Graces more
To Ivy-crowned *Bacchus* bore;
Or whether (as som Sager sing)
The frolick Wind that breathes the Spring,
Zephir with *Aurora* playing,
As he met her once a Maying,   20
There on Beds of Violets blew,
And fresh-blown Roses washt in dew,
Fill'd her with thee a daughter fair,
So bucksom, blith, and debonair.

37

Haste thee nymph, and bring with thee
Jest and youthful Jollity,
Quips and Cranks, and wanton Wiles,
Nods, and Becks, and Wreathed Smiles,
Such as hang on *Hebe*'s cheek,
And love to live in dimple sleek;   30
Sport that wrincled Care derides,
And Laughter holding both his sides.
Com, and trip it as you go
On the light fantastick toe,
And in thy right hand lead with thee,
The Mountain Nymph, sweet Liberty;
And if I give thee honour due,
Mirth, admit me of thy crue
To live with her, and live with thee,
In unreproved pleasures free;
To hear the Lark begin his flight,   40
And singing startle the dull night,
From his watch-towre in the skies,
Till the dappled dawn doth rise;
Then to com in spight of sorrow,
And at my window bid good morrow,
Through the Sweet-Briar, or the Vine,
Or the twisted Eglantine.
While the Cock with lively din,
Scatters the rear of darknes thin,   50
And to the stack, or the Barn dore,
Stoutly struts his Dames before,
Oft list'ning how the Hounds and Horn,
Chearly rouse the slumbring morn,
From the side of som Hoar Hill,
Through the high wood echoing shrill.
Som time walking not unseen
By Hedge-row Elms, on Hillocks green,
Right against the Eastern gate,

Where the great Sun begins his state,   60
Roab'd in flames, and Amber light,
The clouds in thousand Liveries dight,
While the Plowman neer at hand,
Whistles ore the Furrow'd Land,
And the Milkmaid singeth blithe,
And the Mower whets his sithe,
And every Shepherd tells his tale
Under the Hawthorn in the dale.
Streit mine eye hath caught new pleasures
Whilst the Lantskip round it measures,   70
Russet Lawns, and Fallows Gray,
Where the nibling flocks do stray,
Mountains on whose barren brest
The labouring clouds do often rest:
Meadows trim with Daisies pide,
Shallow Brooks, and Rivers wide.
Towers, and Battlements it sees
Boosom'd high in tufted Trees,
Wher perhaps som beauty lies,
The Cynosure of neighbouring eyes.   80
Hard by, a Cottage chimney smokes,
From betwixt two aged Okes,
Where *Corydon* and *Thyrsis* met,
Are at their savory dinner set
Of Hearbs, and other Country Messes,
Which the neat-handed *Phillis* dresses;
And then in haste her Bowre she leaves,
With *Thestylis* to bind the Sheaves;
Or if the earlier season lead
To the tann'd Haycock in the Mead,   90
Some times with secure delight
The up-land Hamlets will invite,
When the merry Bells ring round,
And the jocond rebecks sound

To many a youth, and many a maid,
Dancing in the Chequer'd shade;
And young and old com forth to play
On a Sunshine Holyday,
Till the live-long day-light fail,
Then to the Spicy Nut-brown Ale,   100
With stories told of many a feat,
How *Faery Mab* the junkets eat,
She was pincht, and pull'd she sed,
And by the Friars Lanthorn led
Tells how the drudging *Goblin* swet,
To ern his Cream-bowle duly set,
When in one night, ere glimps of morn,
His shadowy Flale hath thresh'd the Corn,
That ten day-labourers could not end,
Then lies him down the Lubbar Fend.   110
And stretch'd out all the Chimney's length,
Basks at the fire his hairy strength;
And Crop-full out of dores he flings,
Ere the first Cock his Mattin rings.
Thus done the Tales, to bed they creep,
By whispering Winds soon lull'd asleep.
Towred Cities please us then,
And the busie humm of men,
Where throngs of Knights and Barons bold,
In weeds of Peace high triumphs hold,   120
With store of Ladies, whose bright eies
Rain influence, and judge the prise,
Of Wit, or Arms, while both contend
To win her Grace, whom all commend.
There let *Hymen* oft appear
In Saffron robe, with Taper clear,
And pomp, and feast, and revelry,
With mask, and antique Pageantry,
Such sights as youthful Poets dream

On Summer eeves by haunted stream.   130
Then to the well-trod stage anon,
If *Jonsons* learned Sock be on,
Or sweetest *Shakespear* fancies childe,
Warble his native Wood-notes wilde,
And ever against eating Cares,
Lap me in soft *Lydian* Aires,
Married to immortal verse
Such as the meeting soul may pierce
In notes, with many a winding bout
Of lincked sweetness long drawn out,   140
With wanton heed, and giddy cunning,
The melting voice through mazes running;
Untwisting all the chains that ty
The hidden soul of harmony.
That *Orpheus* self may heave his head
From golden slumber on a bed
Of heapt *Elysian* flowres, and hear
Such streins as would have won the ear
Of *Pluto*, to have quite set free
His half regain'd *Eurydice*.   150
These delights, if thou canst give,
Mirth with thee, I mean to live.

[1645]

Il Penseroso.

HENCE vain deluding joyes,
    The brood of folly without father bred,
How little you bested,
    Or fill the fixed mind with all your toyes;
Dwell in some idle brain,

And fancies fond with gaudy shapes possess,
As thick and numberless
   As the gay motes that people the Sun Beams,
Or likest hovering dreams
   The fickle Pensioners of *Morpheus* train.   10
But hail thou Goddess, sage and holy,
Hail divinest Melancholy,
Whose Saintly visage is too bright
To hit the Sense of human sight;
And therefore to our weaker view,
Ore laid with black staid Wisdoms hue.
Black, but such as in esteem,
Prince *Memnons* sister might beseem,
Or that starr'd *Ethiope* Queen that strove
To set her beauties praise above   20
The Sea Nymphs, and their powers offended,
Yet thou art higher far descended,
Thee bright-hair'd *Vesta* long of yore,
To solitary *Saturn* bore;
His daughter she (in *Saturns* raign,
Such mixture was not held a stain)
Oft in glimmering Bowres, and glades
He met her, and in secret shades
Of woody *Ida's* inmost grove,
While yet there was no fear of *Jove*.   30
Com pensive Nun, devout and pure,
Sober, stedfast, and demure,
All in a robe of darkest grain,
Flowing with majestick train,
And sable stole of *Cipres* Lawn,
Over thy decent shoulders drawn.
Com, but keep thy wonted state,
With eev'n step, and musing gate,
And looks commercing with the skies,
Thy rapt soul sitting in thine eyes: 40

There held in holy passion still,
Forget thy self to Marble, till
With a sad Leaden downward cast,
Thou fix them on the earth as fast.
And joyn with thee calm Peace, and Quiet,
Spare Fast, that oft with gods doth diet,
And hears the Muses in a ring,
Ay round about *Joves* Altar sing.
And adde to these retired leasure,
That in trim Gardens takes his pleasure;   50
But first, and chiefest, with thee bring,
Him that yon soars on golden wing,
Guiding the fiery-wheeled throne,
The Cherub Contemplation,
And the mute Silence hist along,
'Less *Philomel* will deign a Song,
In her sweetest, saddest plight,
Smoothing the rugged brow of night,
While *Cynthia* checks her Dragon yoke,
Gently o're th'accustom'd Oke;   60
Sweet Bird that shunn'st the noise of folly,
Most musical, most Melancholy!
Thee Chauntress oft the Woods among,
I woo to hear thy Even-Song;
And missing thee, I walk unseen
On the dry smooth-shaven Green,
To behold the wandring Moon,
Riding neer her highest noon,
Like one that had bin led astray
Through the Heav'ns wide pathles way;   70
And oft, as if her head she bow'd,
Stooping through a fleecy cloud.
Oft on a Plat of rising ground,
I hear the far-off *Curfeu* sound,
Over some wide-water'd shoar,

43

Swinging slow with sullen roar;
Or if the Ayr will not permit,
Som still removed place will fit,
Where glowing Embers through the room
Teach light to counterfeit a gloom,   80
Far from all resort of mirth,
Save the Cricket on the hearth,
Or the Belmans drowsie charm,
To bless the dores from nightly harm:
Or let my Lamp at midnight hour,
Be seen in some high lonely Towr,
Where I may oft out-watch the *Bear*,
With thrice great *Hermes*, or unsphear
The spirit of *Plato* to unfold
What Worlds, or what vast Regions hold   90
The immortal mind that hath forsook
Her mansion in this fleshly nook:
And of those *Dæmons* that are found
In fire, air, flood, or under ground,
Whose power hath a true consent
With Planet, or with Element.
Som time let Gorgeous Tragedy
In Scepter'd Pall com sweeping by,
Presenting *Thebs*, or *Pelops* line,
Or the tale of *Troy* divine.   100
Or what (though rare) of later age,
Ennobled hath the Buskind stage.
But, O sad Virgin, that thy power
Might raise *Musæus* from his bower,
Or bid the soul of *Orpheus* sing
Such notes as warbled to the string,
Drew Iron tears down *Pluto*'s check,
And made Hell grant what Love did seek.
Or call up him that left half told
The story of *Cambuscan* bold,   110

44

Of *Camball*, and of *Algarsife*,
And who had *Canace* to wife,
That own'd the vertuous Ring and Glass,
And of the wondrous Hors of Brass,
On which the *Tartar* King did ride;
And if ought els, great *Bards* beside,
In sage and solemn tunes have sung,
Of Turneys and of Trophies hung;
Of Forests, and inchantments drear,
Where more is meant then meets the ear,   120
Thus night oft see me in thy pale career,
Till civil-suited Morn appeer,
Not trickt and frounc't as she was wont,
With the Attick Boy to hunt,
But Cherchef't in a comely Cloud,
While rocking Winds are Piping loud,
Or usher'd with a shower still,
When the gust hath blown his fill,
Ending on the russling Leaves,
With minute drops from off the Eaves.   130
And when the Sun begins to fling
His flaring beams, me Goddess bring
To arched walks of twilight groves,
And shadows brown that *Sylvan* loves
Of Pine, or monumental Oake,
Where the rude Ax with heaved stroke,
Was never heard the Nymphs to daunt,
Or fright them from their hallow'd haunt.
There in close covert by some Brook,
Where no profaner eye may look,   140
Hide me from Day's garish eie,
While the Bee with Honied thie,
That at her flowry work doth sing,
And the Waters murmuring
With such consort as they keep,

Entice the dewy-feather'd Sleep;
And let som strange mysterious dream,
Wave at his Wings in Airy stream,
Of lively portrature display'd,
Softly on my eye-lids laid.   150
And as I wake, sweet musick breath
Above, about, or underneath,
Sent by som spirit to mortals good,
Or th'unseen Genius of the Wood.
But let my due feet never fail,
To walk the studious Cloysters pale,
And love the high embowed Roof,
With antick Pillars massy proof,
And storied Windows richly dight,
Casting a dimm religious light.   160
There let the pealing Organ blow,
To the full voic'd Quire below,
In Service high, and Anthems cleer,
As may with sweetness, through mine ear,
Dissolve me into extasies,
And bring all Heav'n before mine eyes.
And may at last my weary age
Find out the peacefull hermitage,
The Hairy Gown and Mossy Cell,
Where I may sit and rightly spell,   170
Of every Star that Heav'n doth shew,
And every Herb that sips the dew;
Till old experience do attain
To something like Prophetic strain.
These pleasures *Melancholy* give,
And I with thee will choose to live.

[1645]

46

SONNETS

I.

O Nightingale, that on yon bloomy Spray
    Warbl'st at eeve, when all the Woods are still,
    Thou with fresh hope the Lovers heart dost fill,
    While the jolly hours lead on propitious *May*,
Thy liquid notes that close the eye of Day,
    First heard before the shallow Cuccoo's bill
    Portend success in love; O if *Jove*'s will
    Have linkt that amorous power to thy soft lay,
Now timely sing, ere the rude Bird of Hate
    Foretell my hopeles doom in som Grove ny: 10
    As thou from year to year hast sung too late
For my relief; yet hadst no reason why,
    Whether the Muse, or Love call thee his mate,
    Both them I serve, and of their train am I.

[1645]
[*Sonnets II–VI* are Italian sonnets and are omitted from this edition.]

VII.

How soon hath time the suttle theef of youth,
    Stoln on his wing my three and twentieth yeer!
    My hasting dayes flie on with full career,
    But my late spring no bud or blossom shew'th.
Perhaps my semblance might deceive the truth,
    That I to manhood am arriv'd so near,
    And inward ripenes doth much less appear,
    That som more timely-happy spirits indu'th.
Yet be it less or more, or soon or slow,
    It shall be still in strictest measure eev'n,   10
    To that same lot, however mean or high,
Toward which Time leads me, and the will of Heav'n;

All is, if I have grace to use it so,
As ever in my great task Masters eye.

[1645]

VIII.

Captain or Colonel, or Knight in Arms,
  Whose chance on these defenceless dores may sease,
  If deed of honour did thee ever please,
  Guard them, and him within protect from harms,
He can requite thee, for he knows the charms
  That call Fame on such gentle acts as these,
  And he can spred thy Name o're Lands and Seas,
  What ever clime the Suns bright circle warms.
Lift not thy spear against the Muses Bowre,
  The great *Emathian* Conqueror bid spare   10
  The house of *Pindarus*, when Temple and Towre
Went to the ground: And the repeated air
  Of sad *Electra*'s Poet had the power
  To save th' *Athenian* Walls from ruine bare.

[1645]

VIII:] *Trinity MS. has:* On his dore when the Citty expected an assault *This
is deleted; and the MS. then has:* When the assault was intended to the
Citty

IX.

Lady that in the prime of earliest youth,
  Wisely hast shun'd the broad way and the green,
  And with those few art eminently seen,
  That labour up the Hill of heav'nly Truth,
The better part with *Mary* and with *Ruth*,
  Chosen thou hast, and they that overween,
  And at thy growing vertues fret their spleen,
  No anger find in thee, but pity and ruth.
Thy care is fixt and zealously attends
  To fill thy odorous Lamp with deeds of light,   10
  And Hope that reaps not shame. Therefore be sure

Thou, when the Bridegroom with his feastfull friends
    Passes to bliss at the mid hour of night,
    Hast gain'd thy entrance, Virgin wise and pure.

[1645]

x.

Daughter to that good Earl, once President
    Of *Englands* Counsel, and her Treasury,
    Who liv'd in both, unstain'd with gold or fee,
    And left them both, more in himself content,
Till the sad breaking of that Parlament
    Broke him, as that dishonest victory
    At *Chæronea*, fatal to liberty
    Kill'd with report that Old man eloquent,
Though later born, then to have known the dayes
    Wherin your Father flourisht, yet by you,   10
    Madam, me thinks I see him living yet;
So well your words his noble vertues praise,
    That all both judge you to relate them true,
    And to possess them, Honour'd *Margaret*.

[1645]

XI.

A Book was writ of late call'd *Tetrachordon;*
    And wov'n close, both matter, form and stile;
    The Subject new: it walk'd the Town a while,
    Numbring good intellects; now seldom por'd on.
Crics the stall-reader, bless us! what a word on
    A title page is this! and some in file
    Stand spelling fals, while one might walk to Mile-
    End Green. Why is it harder Sirs then Gordon,
Colkitto, or Macdonnel, or Galasp?
    Those rugged names to our like mouths grow sleek   10
    That would have made *Quintilian* stare and gasp.
Thy age, like ours, O Soul of Sir *John Cheek*,

49

Hated not Learning wors then Toad or Asp;
When thou taught'st *Cambridge*, and King *Edward* Greek.

[1673]

XI] *1673. Trinity MS. has the title:* On the detraction which follow'd upon
my writing certain treatises.

XII. *On the same.*

I did but prompt the age to quit their cloggs
    By the known rules of antient libertie,
    When strait a barbarous noise environs me
Of Owles and Cuckoes, Asses, Apes and Doggs.
As when those Hinds that were transform'd to Froggs
    Raild at *Latona*'s twin-born progenie
    Which after held the Sun and Moon in fee.
But this is got by casting Pearl to Hoggs;
That bawle for freedom in their senceless mood,
    And still revolt when truth would set them free.   10
    Licence they mean when they cry libertie;
For who loves that, must first be wise and good;
    But from that mark how far they roave we see
    For all this wast of wealth, and loss of blood.

[1673]

To Mr. H. Lawes, *on his Aires.*

XIII.

Harry whose tuneful and well measur'd Song
    First taught our English Musick how to span
    Words with just note and accent, not to scan

With *Midas* Ears, committing short and long;
Thy worth and skill exempts thee from the throng,
   With praise enough for Envy to look wan;
   To after age thou shalt be writ the man,
   That with smooth aire couldst humor best our tongue.
Thou honour'st Verse, and Verse must lend her wing
   To honour thee, the Priest of *Phœbus* Quire   10
   That tun'st their happiest lines in Hymn, or Story.
Dante shall give Fame leave to set thee higher
   Then his *Casella*, whom he woo'd to sing
   Met in the milder shades of Purgatory.

[1673]

XIV.

When Faith and Love which parted from thee never,
   Had ripen'd thy just soul to dwell with God,
   Meekly thou didst resign this earthy load
Of Death, call'd Life; which us from Life doth sever.
Thy Works and Alms and all thy good Endeavour
   Staid not behind, nor in the grave were trod;
   But as Faith pointed with her golden rod,
   Follow'd thee up to joy and bliss for ever.
Love led them on, and Faith who knew them best
   Thy hand-maids, clad them o're with purple beams   10
   And azure wings, that up they flew so drest,
And speak the truth of thee on glorious Theams
   Before the Judge, who thenceforth bid thee rest
   And drink thy fill of pure immortal streams.

[1673]

On the Lord Gen. Fairfax at the siege of Colchester.

XV.

Fairfax, whose name in armes through Europe rings
    Filling each mouth with envy, or with praise,
    And all her jealous monarchs with amaze,
    And rumors loud, that daunt remotest kings,
Thy firm unshak'n vertue ever brings
    Victory home, though new rebellions raise
    Thir Hydra heads, & the fals North displaies
    Her brok'n league, to impe their serpent wings,
O yet a nobler task awaites thy hand;
    For what can Warr, but endless warr still breed,   10
    Till Truth, & Right from Violence be freed,
And Public Faith cleard from the shamefull brand
    Of Public Fraud. In vain doth Valour bleed
    While Avarice, & Rapine share the land.

[*Not in 1673. Text and title from Trinity MS.*]

To the Lord Generall Cromwell May 1652.

On the proposalls of certaine ministers at the Commtee for Propagation
of the Gospell.

XVI.

Cromwell, our cheif of men, who through a cloud
    Not of warr onely, but detractions rude,
    Guided by faith & matchless Fortitude
    To peace & truth thy glorious way hast plough'd,
And on the neck of crowned Fortune proud

Hast reard Gods Trophies & his work pursu'd,
While Darwen stream with blood of Scotts imbru'd,
And Dunbarr feild resounds thy praises loud,
And Worsters laureat wreath; yet much remaines
  To conquer still; peace hath her victories   10
  No less renownd then warr, new foes aries
Threatning to bind our soules with secular chaines:
  Helpe us to save free Conscience from the paw
  Of hireling wolves whose Gospell is their maw.

[*Not in 1673. Text and title from Trinity MS.*]

To Sir Henry Vane the younger.

XVII.

Vane, young in yeares, but in sage counsell old,
  Then whome a better Senatour nere held
  The helme of Rome, when gownes not armes repelld
  The feirce Epeirot & the African bold,
Whether to settle peace, or to unfold
  The drift of hollow states, hard to be spelld,
  Then to advise how warr may best, upheld,
  Move by her two maine nerves, Iron & Gold
In all her equipage; besides to know
  Both spirituall powre & civill, what each meanes   10
  What severs each thou 'hast learnt, which few have don.
The bounds of either sword to thee wee ow.
  Therfore on thy firme hand religion leanes
  In peace, & reck'ns thee her eldest son.

[*Not in 1673. Text and title from Trinity MS.*]

XVIII.

Avenge O Lord thy slaughter'd Saints, whose bones
   Lie scatter'd on the Alpine mountains cold,
   Ev'n them who kept thy truth so pure of old
   When all our Fathers worship't Stocks and Stones,
Forget not: in thy book record their groanes
   Who were thy Sheep and in their antient Fold
   Slayn by the bloody *Piemontese* that roll'd
   Mother with Infant down the Rocks. Their moans
The Vales redoubl'd to the Hills, and they
   To Heav'n. Their martyr'd blood and ashes sow   10
   O're all th'*Italian* fields where still doth sway
The triple Tyrant: that from these may grow
   A hunder'd-fold, who having learnt thy way
   Early may fly the *Babylonian* wo.

[1673]

XIX.

When I consider how my light is spent,
   E're half my days, in this dark world and wide,
   And that one Talent which is death to hide,
   Lodg'd with me useless, though my Soul more bent
To serve therewith my Maker, and present
   My true account, least he returning chide,
   Doth God exact day-labour, light deny'd,
   I fondly ask; But patience to prevent
That murmur, soon replies, God doth not need
   Either man's work or his own gifts, who best   10
   Bear his milde yoak, they serve him best, his State
Is Kingly. Thousands at his bidding speed
   And post o're Land and Ocean without rest:
   They also serve who only stand and waite.

[1673]

Lawrence of vertuous Father vertuous Son,
   Now that the Fields are dank, and ways are mire,
   Where shall we sometimes meet, and by the fire
   Help wast a sullen day; what may be won
From the hard Season gaining: time will run
   On smoother, till *Favonius* re-inspire
   The frozen earth; and cloth in fresh attire
The Lillie and Rose, that neither sow'd nor spun.
What neat repast shall feast us, light and choice,
   Of Attick tast, with Wine, whence we may rise   10
   To hear the Lute well toucht, or artfull voice
Warble immortal Notes and *Tuskan* Ayre?
   He who of those delights can judge, And spare
   To interpose them oft, is not unwise.

[1673]

XXI

Cyriack, whose Grandsire on the Royal Bench
   Of Brittish *Themis,* with no mean applause
   Pronounc't and in his volumes taught our Lawes,
   Which others at their Barr so often wrench;
To day deep thoughts resolve with me to drench
   In mirth, that after no repenting drawes;
   Let *Euclid* rest and *Archimedes* pause,
   And what the *Swede* intend, and what the *French*.
To measure life, learn thou betimes, and know
   Toward solid good what leads the nearest way;   10
   For other things mild Heav'n a time ordains,
And disapproves that care, though wise in show,
   That with superfluous burden loads the day,
   And when God sends a cheerful hour, refrains.

[1673]

To Mr. Cyriack Skinner upon his Blindness.

XXII.

Cyriack, this three years day these eys, though clear
    To outward view, of blemish or of spot;
    Bereft of light thir seeing have forgot,
    Nor to thir idle orbs doth sight appear
Of Sun or Moon or Starre throughout the year,
    Or man or woman. Yet I argue not
    Against heavns hand or will, nor bate a jot
    Of heart or hope; but still bear vp and steer
Right onward. What supports me, dost thou ask?
    The conscience, Friend, to have lost them overply'd   10
    In libertyes defence, my noble task,
Of which all Europe talks from side to side.
    This thought might lead me through the world's vain mask
    Content though blind, had I no better guide.

[*Not in 1673. Text from Trinity MS. which has no title. Title from 1694.*]

XXIII.

Methought I saw my late espoused Saint
    Brought to me like *Alcestis* from the grave,
    Whom *Joves* great Son to her glad Husband gave,
    Rescu'd from death by force though pale and faint.
Mine as whom washt from spot of child-bed taint,
    Purification in the old Law did save,
    And such, as yet once more I trust to have
    Full sight of her in Heaven without restraint,
Came vested all in white, pure as her mind:
    Her face was vail'd, yet to my fancied sight,   10
    Love, sweetness, goodness, in her person shin'd
So clear, as in no face with more delight.
    But O as to embrace me she enclin'd
    I wak'd, she fled, and day brought back my night.

[1673]

The Fifth Ode of Horace. Lib. I.

Quis multa gracilis te puer in Rosa, *Rendred almost word for word without Rhyme according to the Latin Measure, as near as the Language will permit.*

What slender Youth bedew'd with liquid odours
Courts thee on Roses in some pleasant Cave,
    Pyrrha for whom bindst thou
    In wreaths thy golden Hair,
Plain in thy neatness; O how oft shall he
On Faith and changed Gods complain: and Seas
    Rough with black winds and storms
    Unwonted shall admire:
Who now enjoyes thee credulous, all Gold,
Who alwayes vacant alwayes amiable   10
    Hopes thee; of flattering gales
    Unmindfull. Hapless they
To whom thou untry'd seem'st fair. Me in my vow'd
Picture the sacred wall declares t' have hung
    My dank and dropping weeds
    To the stern God of Sea.

[1673]
[*The Latin then follows*]

On the new forcers of Conscience under the Long PARLIAMENT.

Because you have thrown of your Prelate Lord,
    And with stiff Vowes renounc'd his Liturgie
    To seise the widdow'd whore Pluralitie
From them whose sin ye envi'd, not abhor'd,

Dare ye for this adjure the Civill Sword
    To force our Consciences that Christ set free,
    And ride us with a classic Hierarchy
    Taught ye by meer *A. S.* and *Rotherford?*
Men whose Life, Learning, Faith and pure intent
    Would have been held in high esteem with *Paul*   10
    Must now be nam'd and printed Hereticks
By shallow *Edwards* and Scotch what d'ye call:
    But we do hope to find out all your tricks,
    Your plots and packing wors then those of *Trent,*
                        That so the Parliament
May with their wholsom and preventive Shears
Clip your Phylacteries, though bauk your Ears,
                        And succour our just Fears
When they shall read this clearly in your charge
New Presbyter is but *Old Priest* writ Large.   20
[1673]

ARCADES.

Part of an Entertainment presented to the Countess Dowager of Darby *at* Hare-
field, *by som Noble Persons of her Family, who appear on the Scene in
Pastoral Habit, moving toward the seat of State, with this Song.*

1. *SONG.*

Look Nymphs, and Shepherds look,
What sudden blaze of Majesty
Is that which we from hence descry
Too divine to be mistook:
    This this is she
To whom our vows and wishes bend,
Heer our solemn search hath end.

Fame that her high worth to raise,
Seem'd erst so lavish and profuse,
We may justly now accuse   10
Of detraction from her praise,
   Less then half we find exprest,
   Envy bid conceal the rest.

Mark what radiant state she spreds,
In circle round her shining throne,
Shooting her beams like silver threds,
This this is she alone,
   Sitting like a Goddes bright,
   In the center of her light.

Might she the wise *Latona* be,   20
Or the towred *Cybele*,
Mother of a hundred gods;
Juno dare's not give her odds;
   Who had thought this clime had held
   A deity so unparalel'd?

As they com forward, the Genius of the Wood appears, and turning toward them, speaks.

   Gen.   Stay gentle Swains, for though in this disguise,
I see bright honour sparkle through your eyes,
Of famous *Arcady* ye are, and sprung
Of that renowned flood, so often sung,
Divine *Alpheus*, who by secret sluse,   30
Stole under Seas to meet his *Arethuse;*
And ye the breathing Roses of the Wood,
Fair silver-buskin'd Nymphs as great and good,
I know this quest of yours, and free intent
Was all in honour and devotion ment
To the great Mistres of yon princely shrine,
Whom with low reverence I adore as mine,

And with all helpful service will comply
To further this nights glad solemnity;
And lead ye where ye may more near behold   40
What shallow-searching *Fame* hath left untold;
Which I full oft amidst these shades alone
Have sate to wonder at, and gaze upon:
For know by lot from *Jove* I am the powr
Of this fair Wood, and live in Oak'n bowr,
To nurse the Saplings tall, and curl the grove
With Ringlets quaint, and wanton windings wove.
And all my Plants I save from nightly ill,
Of noisom winds, and blasting vapours chill.
And from the Boughs brush off the evil dew,   50
And heal the harms of thwarting thunder blew,
Or what the cross dire-looking Planet smites,
Or hurtfull Worm with canker'd venom bites.
When Ev'ning gray doth rise, I fetch my round
Over the mount, and all this hallow'd ground,
And early ere the odorous breath of morn
Awakes the slumbring leaves, or tasseld horn
Shakes the high thicket, haste I all about,
Number my ranks, and visit every sprout
With puissant words, and murmurs made to bless,   60
But els in deep of night when drowsines
Hath lock't up mortal sense, then listen I
To the celestial *Sirens* harmony,
That sit upon the nine enfolded Sphears,
And sing to those that hold the vital shears,
And turn the Adamantine spindle round,
On which the fate of gods and men is wound.
Such sweet compulsion doth in musick ly,
To lull the daughters of *Necessity*,
And keep unsteddy Nature to her law,   70
And the low world in measur'd motion draw
After the heavenly tune, which none can hear

Of human mould with gross unpurged ear;
And yet such musick worthiest were to blaze
The peerles height of her immortal praise,
Whose lustre leads us, and for her most fit,
If my inferior hand or voice could hit
Inimitable sounds, yet as we go,
What ere the skill of lesser gods can show,
I will assay, her worth to celebrate,   80
And so attend ye toward her glittering state;
Where ye may all that are of noble stemm
Approach, and kiss her sacred vestures hemm.

2. *SONG.*

O're the smooth enamel'd green
Where no print of step hath been,
  Follow me as I sing,
  And touch the warbled string.
Under the shady roof
Of branching Elm Star-proof,
  Follow me,   90
I will bring you where she sits
Clad in splendor as befits
  Her deity.
Such a rural Queen
All *Arcadia* hath not seen.

3. *SONG.*

Nymphs and Shepherds dance no more
  By sandy *Ladons* Lillied banks,
On old *Lycæus* or *Cyllene* hoar,
  Trip no more in twilight ranks,
Though *Erymanth* your loss deplore,   100
  A better soyl shall give ye thanks.
From the stony *Mænalus*,
Bring your Flocks, and live with us,

Here ye shall have greater grace,
To serve the Lady of this place.
  Though *Syrinx* your *Pans* Mistress were,
  Yet *Syrinx* well might wait on her.
    Such a rural Queen
    All *Arcadia* hath not seen.

[1645]

LYCIDAS.

In this Monody the Author bewails a learned Friend, unfortunately drown'd in his
passage from Chester *on the* Irish *Seas, 1637. And by occasion foretells the*
ruine of our corrupted Clergy then in their height.

YET once more, O ye Laurels, and once more
Ye Myrtles brown, with Ivy never sear,
I com to pluck your Berries harsh and crude,
And with forc'd fingers rude,
Shatter your leaves before the mellowing year.
Bitter constraint, and sad occasion dear,
Compells me to disturb your season due:
For *Lycidas* is dead, dead ere his prime,
Young *Lycidas*, and hath not left his peer:
Who would not sing for *Lycidas?* he knew   10
Himself to sing, and build the lofty rhyme.
He must not flote upon his watry bear
Unwept, and welter to the parching wind,
Without the meed of som melodious tear.
  Begin then, Sisters of the sacred well,
That from beneath the seat of *Jove* doth spring,
Begin, and somewhat loudly sweep the string.
Hence with denial vain, and coy excuse,

So may some gentle Muse
With lucky words favour my destin'd Urn,   20
And as he passes turn,
And bid fair peace be to my sable shrowd.
For we were nurst upon the self-same hill,
Fed the same flock; by fountain, shade, and rill.
   Together both, ere the high Lawns appear'd
Under the opening eye-lids of the morn,
We drove a field, and both together heard
What time the Gray-fly winds her sultry horn,
Batt'ning our flocks with the fresh dews of night,
Oft till the Star that rose, at Ev'ning, bright,   30
Toward Heav'ns descent had slop'd his westering wheel.
Mean while the Rural ditties were not mute,
Temper'd to th'Oaten Flute,
Rough *Satyrs* danc'd, and *Fauns* with clov'n heel,
From the glad sound would not be absent long,
And old *Damœtas* lov'd to hear our song.
   But O the heavy change, now thou art gon,
Now thou art gon, and never must return!
Thee Shepherd, thee the Woods, and desert Caves,
With wilde Thyme and the gadding Vine o'regrown,   40
And all their echoes mourn.
The Willows, and the Hazle Copses green,
Shall now no more be seen,
Fanning their joyous Leaves to thy soft layes.
As killing as the Canker to the Rose,
Or Taint-worm to the weanling Herds that graze,
Or Frost to Flowers, that their gay wardrop wear,
When first the White thorn blows;
Such, *Lycidas*, thy loss to Shepherds ear.
   Where were ye Nymphs when the remorseless deep   50
Clos'd o're the head of your lov'd *Lycidas*?
For neither were ye playing on the steep,
Where your old *Bards*, the famous *Druids*, ly,

Nor on the shaggy top of *Mona* high,
Nor yet where *Deva* spreads her wisard stream:
Ay me, I fondly dream!
Had ye bin there—for what could that have don?
What could the Muse her self that *Orpheus* bore,
The Muse her self, for her inchanting son
Whom Universal nature did lament,   60
When by the rout that made the hideous roar,
His goary visage down the stream was sent,
Down the swift *Hebrus* to the *Lesbian* shore.

  Alas! What boots it with uncessant care
To tend the homely slighted Shepherds trade,
And strictly meditate the thankless Muse,
Were it not better don as others use,
To sport with *Amaryllis* in the shade,
Or with the tangles of *Neæra's* hair?
Fame is the spur that the clear spirit doth raise   70
(That last infirmity of Noble mind)
To scorn delights, and live laborious dayes;
But the fair Guerdon when we hope to find,
And think to burst out into sudden blaze,
Comes the blind *Fury* with th'abhorred shears,
And slits the thin-spun life. But not the praise,
Phœbus repli'd, and touch'd my trembling ears;
Fame is no plant that grows on mortal soil,
Nor in the glistering foil
Set off to th'world, nor in broad rumour lies,   80

58–63 What could . . . Lesbian shore. *Trinity MS first reads:* what could the
   golden haryd Calliope/ for her inchaunting son/ when shee beheld (the
   gods farre sighted bee) /his goarie scalpe rowle downe the Thracian lee.
   The last two lines of this were then deleted and rewritten: whome universal
   nature might lament/ and heaven and hel deplore/ whenn his divine
   head downe the stream was sent/ downe the swift Hebrus to the
   Lesbian shore.

But lives and spreds aloft by those pure eyes,
And perfet witnes of all-judging *Jove;*
As he pronounces lastly on each deed,
Of so much fame in Heav'n expect thy meed.

O Fountain *Arethuse*, and thou honour'd floud,
Smooth-sliding *Mincius*, crown'd with vocal reeds,
That strain I heard was of a higher mood:
But now my Oat proceeds,
And listens to the Herald of the Sea
That came in *Neptune*'s plea,   90
He ask'd the Waves, and ask'd the Fellon Winds,
What hard mishap hath doom'd this gentle swain?
And question'd every gust of rugged wings
That blows from off each beaked Promontory;
They knew not of his story,
And sage *Hippotades* their answer brings,
That not a blast was from his dungeon stray'd,
The Ayr was calm, and on the level brine,
Sleek *Panope* with all her sisters play'd.
It was that fatal and perfidious Bark   100
Built in th'eclipse, and rigg'd with curses dark,
That sunk so low that sacred head of thine.

Next *Camus*, reverend Sire, went footing slow,
His Mantle hairy, and his Bonnet sedge,
Inwrought with figures dim, and on the edge
Like to that sanguine flower inscrib'd with woe.
Ah; Who hath reft (quoth he) my dearest pledge?
Last came, and last did go,
The Pilot of the *Galilean* lake,
Two massy Keyes he bore of metals twain,   110
(The Golden opes, the Iron shuts amain)
He shook his Miter'd locks, and stern bespake,
How well could I have spar'd for thee, young swain,
Anow of such as for their bellies sake,
Creep and intrude, and climb into the fold?

Of other care they little reck'ning make,
Then how to scramble at the shearers feast,
And shove away the worthy bidden guest;
Blind mouthes! that scarce themselves know how to hold
A Sheep-hook, or have learn'd ought els the least   120
That to the faithfull Herdmans art belongs!
What recks it them? What need they? They are sped;
And when they list, their lean and flashy songs
Grate on their scrannel Pipes of wretched straw,
The hungry Sheep look up, and are not fed,
But swoln with wind, and the rank mist they draw,
Rot inwardly, and foul contagion spread:
Besides what the grim Woolf with privy paw
Daily devours apace, and nothing sed,
But that two-handed engine at the door,   130
Stands ready to smite once, and smite no more.
     Return *Alpheus*, the dread voice is past,
That shrunk thy streams; Return *Sicilian* Muse,
And call the Vales, and bid them hither cast
Their Bells, and Flourets of a thousand hues.
Ye valleys low where the milde whispers use,
Of shades and wanton winds, and gushing brooks,
On whose fresh lap the swart Star sparely looks,
Throw hither all your quaint enameld eyes,
That on the green terf suck the honied showres,   140
And purple all the ground with vernal flowres.
Bring the rathe Primrose that forsaken dies.
The tufted Crow-toe, and pale Gessamine,
The white Pink, and the Pansie freakt with jeat,
The glowing Violet,
The Musk-rose, and the well attir'd Woodbine,
With Cowslips wan that hang the pensive head,
And every flower that sad embroidery wears:
Bid *Amaranthus* all his beauty shed,
And Daffadillies fill their cups with tears,   150

To strew the Laureat Herse where *Lycid* lies.
For so to interpose a little ease,
Let our frail thoughts dally with false surmise.
Ay me! Whilst thee the shores, and sounding Seas
Wash far away, where ere thy bones are hurl'd,
Whether beyond the stormy *Hebrides*
Where thou perhaps under the whelming tide
Visit'st the bottom of the monstrous world;
Or whether thou to our moist vows deny'd,
Sleep'st by the fable of *Bellerus* old,   160
Where the great vision of the guarded Mount
Looks toward *Namancos* and *Bayona*'s hold;
Look homeward Angel now, and melt with ruth.
And, O ye *Dolphins*, waft the haples youth.
   Weep no more, woful Shepherds weep no more,
For *Lycidas* your sorrow is not dead,
Sunk though he be beneath the watry floar,
So sinks the day-star in the Ocean bed,
And yet anon repairs his drooping head,
And tricks his beams, and with new spangled Ore,   170
Flames in the forehead of the morning sky:
So *Lycidas* sunk low, but mounted high,
Through the dear might of him that walk'd the waves
Where other groves, and other streams along,
With *Nectar* pure his oozy Lock's he laves,
And hears the unexpressive nuptial Song,
In the blest Kingdoms meek of joy and love.
There entertain him all the Saints above,
In solemn troops, and sweet Societies
That sing, and singing in their glory move,   180
And wipe the tears for ever from his eyes.
Now *Lycidas* the Shepherds weep no more;
Henceforth thou art the Genius of the shore,
In thy large recompense, and shalt be good
To all that wander in that perilous flood.

Thus sang the uncouth Swain to th'Okes and rills,
While the still morn went out with Sandals gray,
He touch'd the tender stops of various Quills,
With eager thought warbling his *Dorick* lay:
And now the Sun had stretch'd out all the hills,   190
And now was dropt into the Western Bay;
At last he rose, and twitch'd his Mantle blew:
To morrow to fresh Woods, and Pastures new.

[1645]

A MASK PRESENTED
At LUDLOW-CASTLE, 1634. *&c.*

[COMUS]

The first Scene discovers a wilde Wood.
The attendant Spirit descends or enters.

BEFORE the starry threshold of *Joves* Court
My mansion is, where those immortal shapes
Of bright aereal Spirits live insphear'd
In Regions milde of calm and serene Air,
Above the smoak and stirr of this dim spot,
Which men call Earth, and with low-thoughted care
Confin'd, and pester'd in this pin-fold here,
Strive to keep up a frail, and Feaverish being
Unmindfull of the crown that Vertue gives
After this mortal change, to her true Servants   10
Amongst the enthron'd gods on Sainted seats.
Yet som there be that by due steps aspire
To lay their just hands on that Golden Key
That ope's the Palace of Eternity:
To such my errand is, and but for such,
I would not soil these pure Ambrosial weeds,

68

With the rank vapours of this Sin-worn mould.
   But to my task. *Neptune* besides the sway
Of every salt Flood, and each ebbing Stream,
Took in by lot 'twixt high, and neather *Jove*,   20
Imperial rule of all the Sea-girt Iles
That like to rich, and various gemms inlay
The unadorned boosom of the Deep,
Which he to grace his tributary gods
By course commits to several government,
And gives them leave to wear their Saphire crowns,
And weild their little tridents, but this Ile
The greatest, and the best of all the main
He quarters to his blu-hair'd deities,
And all this tract that fronts the falling Sun   30
A noble Peer of mickle trust, and power
Has in his charge, with temper'd awe to guide
An old, and haughty Nation proud in Arms:
Where his fair off-spring nurs't in Princely lore,
Are coming to attend their Fathers state,
And new-entrusted Scepter, but their way
Lies through the perplex't paths of this drear Wood,
The nodding horror of whose shady brows
Threats the forlorn and wandring Passinger.
And here their tender age might suffer peril,   40
But that by quick command from Soveran *Jove*
I was dispatcht for their defence, and guard;
And listen why, for I will tell ye now   *New story*
What never yet was heard in Tale or Song
From old, or modern Bard in Hall, or Bowr.
   Bacchus that first from out the purple Grape,
Crush't the sweet poyson of mis-used Wine
After the *Tuscan* Mariners transform'd
Coasting the *Tyrrhene* shore, as the winds listed,
On *Circes* Iland fell (who knows not *Circe*   50
The daughter of the Sun? Whose charmed Cup

69

Whoever tasted, lost his upright shape,
And downward fell into a groveling Swine)
This Nymph that gaz'd upon his clustring locks,
With Ivy berries wreath'd, and his blithe youth,
Had by him, ere he parted thence, a Son
Much like his Father, but his Mother more,
Whom therefore she brought up and *Comus* nam'd,
Who ripe, and frolick of his full grown age,
Roaving the *Celtick*, and *Iberian* fields,   60
At last betakes him to this ominous Wood,
And in thick shelter of black shades imbowr'd,
Excells his Mother at her mighty Art,
Offring to every weary Traveller,
His orient Liquor in a Crystal Glass,
To quench the drouth of *Phœbus*, which as they taste
(For most do taste through fond intemperate thirst) .
Soon as the Potion works, their human count'nance,
Th' express resemblance of the gods, is chang'd
Into som brutish form of Woolf, or Bear,   70
Or Ounce, or Tiger, Hog, or bearded Goat,
All other parts remaining as they were,
And they, so perfect is their misery,
Not once perceive their foul disfigurement,
But boast themselves more comely then before
And all their friends, and native home forget
To roule with pleasure in a sensual stie.
Therfore when any favour'd of high *Jove*,
Chances to passe through this adventrous glade,
Swift as the Sparkle of a glancing Star,   80
I shoot from Heav'n to give him safe convoy,
As now I do: But first I must put off
These my skie robes spun out of *Iris* Wooff,
And take the Weeds and likenes of a Swain,
That to the service of this house belongs,
Who with his soft Pipe, and smooth dittied Song,

Well knows to still the wilde winds when they roar,
And hush the waving Woods, nor of less faith,
And in this office of his Mountain watch,
Likeliest, and nearest to the present ayd   90
Of this occasion. But I hear the tread
Of hatefull steps, I must be viewles now.

*Comus enters with a Charming Rod in one hand, his Glass in the other, with
    him a rout of Monsters, headed like sundry sorts of wilde Beasts, but otherwise
    like Men and Women, their Apparel glistering, they come in making a
    riotous and unruly noise, with Torches in their hands.*

  Comus. The Star that bids the Shepherd fold,
Now the top of Heav'n doth hold,
And the gilded Car of Day,
His glowing Axle doth allay
In the steep *Atlantick* stream,
And the slope Sun his upward beam
Shoots against the dusky Pole,
Pacing toward the other gole   100
Of his Chamber in the East.
Mean while welcom Joy, and Feast,
Midnight shout, and revelry,
Tipsie dance, and Jollity.
Braid your Locks with rosie Twine
Dropping odours, dropping Wine.
Rigor now is gon to bed,
And Advice with scrupulous head,
Strict Age, and sowre Severity.
With their grave Saws in slumber lie.   110
We that are of purer fire
Imitate the Starry Quire,
Who in their nightly watchfull Sphears,
Lead in swift round the Months and Years.
The Sounds, and Seas with all their finny drove
Now to the Moon in wavering Morrice move,

And on the Tawny Sands and Shelves,
Trip the pert Fairies and the dapper Elves;
By dimpled Brook, and Fountain brim,
The Wood-Nymphs deckt with Daisies trim, 120
Their merry wakes and pastimes keep:
What hath night to do with sleep?
Night hath better sweets to prove,
Venus now wakes, and wak'ns Love.
Com let us our rights begin,
Tis onely day-light that makes Sin
Which these dun shades will ne're report.
Hail Goddess of Nocturnal sport
Dark vail'd *Cotytto*, t' whom the secret flame
Of mid-night Torches burns; mysterious Dame 130
That ne're art call'd, but when the Dragon woom
Of Stygian darkness spets her thickest gloom,
And makes one blot of all the air,
Stay thy cloudy Ebon chair,
Wherin thou rid'st with *Heccat'*, and befriend
Us thy vow'd Priests, till utmost end
Of all thy dues be done, and none left out,
Ere the blabbing Eastern scout,
The nice Morn on th' *Indian* steep
From her cabin'd loop-hole peep, 140
And to the tell-tale Sun discry
Our conceal'd Solemnity.
Com, knit hands, and beat the ground,
In a light fantastick round.

The Measure.

Break off, break off, I feel the different pace,
Of som chast footing near about this ground.
Run to your shrouds, within these Brakes and Trees,
Our number may affright: Som Virgin sure
(For so I can distinguish by mine Art)

72

Benighted in these Woods. Now to my charms,   150
And to my wily trains, I shall e're long
Be well stock't with as fair a herd as graz'd
About my Mother *Circe*. Thus I hurl
My dazling Spells into the spungy ayr,
Of power to cheat the eye with blear illusion,
And give it false presentments, lest the place
And my quaint habits breed astonishment,
And put the Damsel to suspicious flight,
Which must not be, for that's against my course;
I under fair pretence of friendly ends,   160
And well plac't words of glozing courtesie
Baited with reasons not unplausible
Wind me into the easie-hearted man,
And hugg him into snares. When once her eye
Hath met the vertue of this Magick dust,
I shall appear som harmles Villager
And hearken, if I may her, busines here.
But here she comes, I fairly step aside.

                    The Lady enters.

This way the noise was, if mine ear be true,
My best guide now, me thought it was the sound   170
Of Riot, and ill manag'd Merriment,
Such as the jocond Flute, or gamesom Pipe
Stirs up among the loose unletter'd Hinds,
When for their teeming Flocks, and granges full
In wanton dance they praise the bounteous *Pan*,
And thank the gods amiss. I should be loath
To meet the rudeness, and swill'd insolence
Of such late Wassailers; yet O where els
Shall I inform my unacquainted feet
In the blind mazes of this tangl'd Wood?   180
My Brothers when they saw me wearied out
With this long, way, resolving here to lodge

                        73

Under the spreading favour of these Pines,
Stept as they se'd to the next Thicket side
To bring me Berries, or such cooling fruit
As the kind hospitable Woods provide.
They left me then, when the gray-hooded Eev'n
Like a sad Votarist in Palmers weed
Rose from the hindmost wheels of *Phœbus* wain.
But where they are, and why they came not back,   190
Is now the labour of my thoughts, 'tis likeliest
They had ingag'd their wandring steps too far,
And envious darknes, e're they could return,
Had stole them from me, els O theevish Night
Why shouldst thou, but for som fellonious end,
In thy dark Lantern thus close up the Stars,
That nature hung in Heav'n, and fill'd their Lamps
With everlasting oil, to give due light
To the misled and lonely Traveller?
This is the place, as well as I may guess,   200
Whence eev'n now the tumult of loud Mirth
Was rife, and perfet in my list'ning ear,
Yet nought but single darknes do I find.
What might this be? A thousand fantasies
Begin to throng into my memory
Of calling shapes, and beckning shadows dire,
And airy tongues, that syllable mens names
On Sands, and Shoars, and desert Wildernesses.
These thoughts may startle well, but not astound
The vertuous mind, that ever walks attended   210
By a strong siding champion Conscience.——
O welcom pure-ey'd Faith, white-handed Hope,
Thou hovering Angel girt with golden wings,
And thou unblemish't form of Chastity,
I see ye visibly, and now beleeve
That he, the Supreme good, t' whom all things ill
Are but as slavish officers of vengeance,

Would send a glistring Guardian if need were
To keep my life and honour unassail'd.
Was I deceiv'd, or did a sable cloud   220
Turn forth her silver lining on the night?
I did not err, there does a sable cloud
Turn forth her silver lining on the night,
And casts a gleam over this tufted Grove.
I cannot hallow to my Brothers, but
Such noise as I can make to be heard farthest
Ile venter, for my new enliv'nd spirits
Prompt me; and they perhaps are not far off.

SONG.

Sweet Echo, sweetest Nymph that liv'st unseen
*   Within thy airy shell*   230
*   By slow Meander's margent green,*
* And in the violet imbroider'd vale*
*   Where the love-lorn Nightingale*
Nightly to thee her sad Song mourneth well.
Canst thou not tell me of a gentle Pair
*   That likest thy Narcissus are?*
*   O if thou have*
*   Hid them in som flowry Cave,*
*   Tell me but where*
Sweet Queen of Parly, Daughter of the Sphear,   240
* So maist thou be translated to the skies,*
And give resounding grace to all Heav'ns Harmonies.

Com. Can any mortal mixture of Earths mould
Breath such Divine inchanting ravishment?
Sure somthing holy lodges in that brest,
And with these raptures moves the vocal air
To testifie his hidd'n residence;

How sweetly did they float upon the wings
Of silence, through the empty-vaulted night
At every fall smoothing the Raven doune   250
Of darknes till it smil'd: I have oft heard
My mother *Circe* with the Sirens three,
Amid'st the flowry-kirtl'd *Naiades*
Culling their Potent hearbs, and balefull drugs,
Who as they sung, would take the prison'd soul,
And lap it in *Elysium*, *Scylla* wept,
And chid her barking waves into attention,
And fell *Charybdis* murmur'd soft applause:
Yet they in pleasing slumber lull'd the sense,
And in sweet madnes rob'd it of it self,   260
But such a sacred, and home-felt delight,
Such sober certainty of waking bliss
I never heard till now. Ile speak to her
And she shall be my Queen. Hail forren wonder
Whom certain these rough shades did never breed
Unless the Goddes that in rural shrine
Dwell'st here with *Pan*, or *Silvan*, by blest Song
Forbidding every bleak unkindly Fog
To touch the prosperous growth of this tall Wood.
   La. Nay gentle Shepherd ill is lost that praise   270
That is addrest to unattending Ears,
Not any boast of skill, but extreme shift
How to regain my sever'd company
Compell'd me to awake the courteous Echo
To give me answer from her mossie Couch.
   Co. What chance good Lady hath bereft you thus?
   La. Dim darknes, and this leavie Labyrinth.
   Co. Could that divide you from neer-ushering guides?
   La. They left me weary on a grassie terf.
   Co. By falshood, or discourtesie, or why?   280
   La. To seek i'th vally som cool friendly Spring.
   Co. And left your fair side all unguarded Lady?

76

La. They were but twain, and purpos'd quick return.
Co. Perhaps fore-stalling night prevented them.
La. How easie my misfortune is to hit!
Co. Imports their loss, beside the present need?
La. No less then if I should my brothers loose.
Co. Were they of manly prime, or youthful bloom?
La. As smooth as *Hebe*'s their unrazor'd lips.
Co. Two such I saw, what time the labour'd Oxe   290
In his loose traces from the furrow came,
And the swink't hedger at his Supper sate;
I saw them under a green mantling vine
That crawls along the side of yon small hill,
Plucking ripe clusters from the tender shoots,
Their port was more then human, as they stood;
I took it for a faëry vision
Of som gay creatures of the element
That in the colours of the Rainbow live
And play i'th plighted clouds. I was aw-strook,   300
And as I past, I worshipt; if those you seek
It were a journey like the path to Heav'n,
To help you find them. *La.* Gentle villager
What readiest way would bring me to that place?
   Co. Due west it rises from this shrubby point.
   La. To find out that, good Shepherd, I suppose,
In such a scant allowance of Star-light,
Would overtask the best Land-Pilots art,
Without the sure guess of well-practiz'd feet.
   Co. I know each lane, and every alley green   310
Dingle, or bushy dell of this wilde Wood,
And every bosky bourn from side to side
My daily walks and ancient neighbourhood,
And if your stray attendance be yet lodg'd,
Or shroud within these limits, I shall know
Ere morrow wake, or the low roosted lark
From her thatch't pallat rowse, if otherwise

I can conduct you Lady to a low
But loyal cottage, where you may be safe
Till further quest. *La.* Shepherd I take thy word,   320
And trust thy honest offer'd courtesie,
Which oft is sooner found in lowly sheds
With smoaky rafters, then in tapstry Halls
And Courts of Princes, where it first was nam'd,
And yet is most pretended: In a place
Less warranted then this, or less secure
I cannot be, that I should fear to change it,
Eie me blest Providence, and square my triall
To my proportion'd strength. Shepherd lead on.——

The two Brothers.

Eld. Bro. Unmuffle ye faint Stars, and thou fair Moon   330
That wontst to love the travellers benizon,
Stoop thy pale visage through an amber cloud,
And disinherit *Chaos*, that raigns here
In double night of darkness, and of shades;
Or if your influence be quite damm'd up
With black usurping mists, som gentle taper
Though a rush Candle from the wicker hole
Of som clay habitation visit us
With thy long levell'd rule of streaming light,
And thou shalt be our star of *Arcady*,   340
Or *Tyrian* Cynosure. *2. Bro.* Or if our eyes
Be barr'd that happines, might we but hear
The folded flocks pen'd in their watled cotes,
Or sound of pastoral reed with oaten stops,
Or whistle from the Lodge, or Village Cock
Count the night watches to his feathery Dames,
'Twould be som solace yet som little chearing
In this close dungeon of innumerous bowes.
But O that haples virgin our lost sister
Where may she wander now, whether betake her   350

78

From the chill dew, amongst rude burrs and thistles?
Perhaps som cold bank is her boulster now
Or 'gainst the rugged bark of som broad Elm
Leans her unpillow'd head fraught with sad fears,
What if in wild amazement, and affright,
Or while we speak within the direful grasp
Of Savage hunger, or of Savage heat?
   Eld. Bro. Peace Brother, be not over-exquisite
To cast the fashion of uncertain evils;
For grant they be so, while they rest unknown,   360
What need a man forestall his date of grief,
And run to meet what he would most avoid?
Or if they be but false alarms of Fear,
How bitter is such self-delusion?
I do not think my sister so to seek,
Or so unprincipl'd in vertues book,
And the sweet peace that goodnes boosoms ever,
As that the single want of light and noise
(Not being in danger, as I trust she is not)
Could stir the constant mood of her calm thoughts,   370
And put them into mis-becoming plight.
Vertue could see to do what vertue would
By her own radiant light, though Sun and Moon
Were in the flat Sea sunk. And Wisdoms self
Oft seeks to sweet retired Solitude,
Where with her best nurse Contemplation
She plumes her feathers, and lets grow her wings
That in the various bussle of resort
Were all to ruffl'd, and somtimes impair'd.
He that has light within his own cleer brest   380
May sit i'th center, and enjoy bright day,
But he that hides a dark soul, and foul thoughts
Benighted walks under the mid-day Sun;
Himself is his own dungeon.
   2. *Bro.* Tis most true

That musing meditation most affects
The pensive secrecy of desert cell,
Far from the cheerfull haunt of men, and herds,
And sits as safe as in a Senat house,
For who would rob a Hermit of his Weeds,
His few Books, or his Beads, or Maple Dish,   390
Or do his gray hairs any violence?
But beauty like the fair Hesperian Tree
Laden with blooming gold, had need the guard
Of dragon watch with uninchanted eye,
To save her blossoms, and defend her fruit
From the rash hand of bold Incontinence.
You may as well spred out the unsun'd heaps
Of Misers treasure by an out-laws den,
And tell me it is safe, as bid me hope
Danger will wink on Opportunity,   400
And let a single helpless maiden pass
Uninjur'd in this wilde surrounding wast.
Of night, or loneliness it recks me not,
I fear the dred events that dog them both,
Lest som ill greeting touch attempt the person
Of our unowned sister.
   Eld. Bro. I do not, Brother,
Inferr, as if I thought my sisters state
Secure without all doubt, or controversie:
Yet where an equal poise of hope and fear
Does arbitrate th'event, my nature is   410
That I encline to hope, rather then fear,
And gladly banish squint suspicion.
My sister is not so defenceless left
As you imagine, she has a hidden strength
Which you remember not.
   2. *Bro.* What hidden strength,
Unless the strength of Heav'n, if you mean that?
   Eld. Bro. I mean that too, but yet a hidden strength

Which if Heav'n gave it, may be term'd her own:
'Tis chastity, my brother, chastity:
She that has that, is clad in compleat steel,   420
And like a quiver'd Nymph with Arrows keen
May trace huge Forrests, and unharbour'd Heaths,
Infamous Hills, and sandy perilous wildes,
Where through the sacred rayes of Chastity,
No savage fierce, Bandite, or Mountaneer
Will dare to soyl her Virgin purity,
Yea there, where very desolation dwels
By grots, and caverns shag'd with horrid shades,
She may pass on with unblench't majesty,
Be it not don in pride, or in presumption.   430
Som say no evil thing that walks by night
In fog, or fire, by lake, or moorish fen,
Blew meager Hag, or stubborn unlaid ghost,
That breaks his magick chains at *curfeu* time,
No Goblin, or swart Faëry of the mine,
Hath hurtfull power o're true Virginity.
Do ye believe me yet, or shall I call
Antiquity from the old Schools of *Greece*
To testifie the arms of Chastity?
Hence had the huntress *Dian* her dred bow   440
Fair silver-shafted Queen for ever chaste,
Wherwith she tam'd the brinded lioness
And spotted mountain pard, but set at nought
The frivolous bolt of *Cupid*, gods and men
Fear'd her stern frown, and she was queen oth' Woods.
What was that snaky-headed *Gorgon* sheild
That wise *Minerva* wore, unconquer'd Virgin,
Wherwith she freez'd her foes to congeal'd stone?
But rigid looks of Chast austerity,
And noble grace that dash't brute violence   450
With sudden adoration, and blank aw.
So dear to Heav'n is Saintly chastity,

That when a soul is found sincerely so,
A thousand liveried Angels lacky her,
Driving far off each thing of sin and guilt,
And in cleer dream, and solemn vision
Tell her of things that no gross ear can hear,
Till oft convers with heav'nly habitants
Begin to cast a beam on th'outward shape,
The unpolluted temple of the mind,   460
And turns it by degrees to the souls essence,
Till all be made immortal: but when lust
By unchaste looks, loose gestures, and foul talk,
But most by leud and lavish act of sin,
Lets in defilement to the inward parts,
The soul grows clotted by contagion,
Imbodies, and imbrutes, till she quite loose
The divine property of her first being.
Such are those thick and gloomy shadows damp
Oft seen in Charnel vaults, and Sepulchers   470
Lingering, and sitting by a new made grave,
As loath to leave the body that it lov'd,
And link't it self by carnal sensuality
To a degenerate and degraded state.
   2. *Bro.* How charming is divine Philosophy!
Not harsh, and crabbed as dull fools suppose,
But musical as is *Apollo*'s lute,
And a perpetual feast of nectar'd sweets,
Where no crude surfet raigns. *Eld. Bro.* List, list, I hear
Som far of hallow break the silent Air.   480
   2. *Bro.* Me thought so too; what should it be?
   Eld. Bro. For certain
Either som one like us night-founder'd here,
Or els som neighbour Wood-man, or at worst,
Some roaving Robber calling to his fellows.
   2. *Bro.* Heav'n keep my sister, agen, agen, and neer,
Best draw, and stand upon our guard.

Eld. Bro. Ile hallow,
If he be friendly he comes well, if not,
Defence is a good cause, and Heav'n be for us.

The attendant Spirit habited like a Shepherd.

That hallow I should know, what are you? speak;
Com not too neer, you fall on iron stakes else.   490
   Spir. What voice is that, my young Lord? speak agen.
   2. *Bro.* O brother, 'tis my father Shepherd sure.
   Eld. Bro. Thyrsis? Whose artful strains have oft delaid
The hudling brook to hear his madrigal,
And sweetn'd every muskrose of the dale,
How cam'st thou here good Swain? hath any Ram
Slipt from the fold, or young Kid lost his dam,
Or straggling Weather the pen't flock forsook?
How couldst thou find this dark sequester'd nook?
   Spir. O my lov'd Masters heir, and his next joy,   500
I came not here on such a trivial toy
As a stray'd Ewe, or to pursue the stealth
Of pilfering Woolf, not all the fleecy wealth
That doth enrich these Downs, is worth a thought
To this my errand, and the care it brought.
But O my Virgin Lady, where is she?
How chance she is not in your company?
   Eld. Bro. To tell thee sadly Shepherd, without blame,
Or our neglect, we lost her as we came.
   Spir. Ay me unhappy then my fears are true.   510
   Eld. Bro. What fears good *Thyrsis?* Prethee briefly shew.
   Spir. Ile tell ye, 'tis not vain, or fabulous,
(Though so esteem'd by shallow ignorance)
What the sage Poëts taught by th' heav'nly Muse,
Storied of old in high immortal vers
Of dire *Chimera's* and inchanted Iles,
And rifted Rocks whose entrance leads to Hell,
For such there be, but unbelief is blind.

Within the navil of this hideous Wood,
Immur'd in cypress shades a Sorcerer dwels 520
Of *Bacchus*, and of *Circe* born, great *Comus*,
Deep skill'd in all his mothers witcheries,
And here to every thirsty wanderer,
By sly enticement gives his baneful cup,
With many murmurs mixt, whose pleasing poison
The visage quite transforms of him that drinks,
And the inglorious likenes of a beast
Fixes instead, unmoulding reasons mintage
Character'd in the face; this have I learn't
Tending my flocks hard by i'th hilly crofts, 530
That brow this bottom glade, whence night by night
He and his monstrous rout are heard to howl
Like stabl'd wolves, or tigers at their prey,
Doing abhorred rites to *Hecate*
In their obscured haunts of inmost bowres,
Yet have they many baits, and guilefull spells
To inveigle and invite th'unwary sense
Of them that pass unweeting by the way.
This evening late by then the chewing flocks
Had ta'n their supper on the savoury Herb 540
Of Knot-grass dew-besprent, and were in fold,
I sate me down to watch upon a bank
With Ivy canopied, and interwove
With flaunting Hony-suckle, and began
Wrapt in a pleasing fit of melancholy
To mediate upon my rural minstrelsie,
Till fancy had her fill, but ere a close
The wonted roar was up amidst the Woods,
And fill'd the Air with barbarous dissonance
At which I ceas't, and listen'd them a while, 550
Till an unusuall stop of sudden silence
Gave respit to the drowsie frighted steeds
That draw the litter of close-curtain'd sleep;

At last a soft and solemn breathing sound
Rose like a steam of rich distill'd perfumes,
And stole upon the Air, that even Silence
Was took e're she was ware, and wisht she might
Deny her nature, and be never more
Still to be so displac't. I was all ear,
And took in strains that might create a soul   560
Under the ribs of Death, but O ere long
Too well I did perceive it was the voice
Of my most honour'd Lady, your dear sister.
Amaz'd I stood, harrow'd with grief and fear,
And O poor hapless Nightingale thought I,
How sweet thou sing'st, how near the deadly snare!
Then down the Lawns I ran with headlong hast
Through paths, and turnings oft'n trod by day,
Till guided by mine ear I found the place
Where that damn'd wisard hid in sly disguise   570
(For so by certain signes I knew) had met
Already, ere my best speed could prævent,
The aidless innocent Lady his wish't prey,
Who gently ask't if he had seen such two,
Supposing him som neighbour villager;
Longer I durst not stay, but soon I guess't
Ye were the two she mean't, with that I sprung
Into swift flight, till I had found you here,
But furder know I not. 2. *Bro.* O night and shades,
How are ye joyn'd with Hell in tripple knot   580
Against th'unarmed weakness of one Virgin
Alone, and helpless! is this the confidence
You gave me Brother? *Eld. Bro.* Yes, and keep it still,
Lean on it safely, not a period
Shall be unsaid for me: against the threats
Of malice or of sorcery, or that power
Which erring men call Chance, this I hold firm,
Vertue may be assail'd, but never hurt,

85

Surpriz'd by unjust force, but not enthrall'd,
Yea even that which mischief meant most harm, 590
Shall in the happy trial prove most glory.
But evil on it self shall back recoyl,
And mix no more with goodness, when at last
Gather'd like scum, and setl'd to it self
It shall be in eternal restless change
Self-fed, and self-consum'd, if this fail,
The pillar'd firmament is rott'nness,
And earths base built on stubble. But com let's on.
Against th' opposing will and arm of Heav'n
May never this just sword be lifted up, 600
But for that damn'd Magician, let him be girt
With all the greisly legions that troop
Under the sooty flag of *Acheron*,
Harpyes and *Hydra*'s, or all the monstrous forms
'Twixt *Africa* and *Inde*, Ile find him out,
And force him to restore his purchase back,
Or drag him by the curls, to a foul death,
Curs'd as his life.
    Spir. Alas good ventrous youth,
I love thy courage yet, and bold Emprise,
But here thy sword can do thee little stead, 610
Far other arms, and other weapons must
Be those that quell the might of hellish charms,
He with his bare wand can unthred thy joynts,
And crumble all thy sinews.
    Eld. Bro. Why prethee Shepherd
How durst thou then thy self approach so neer
As to make this Relation?
    Spir. Care and utmost shifts
How to secure the Lady from surprisal,
Brought to my mind a certain Shepherd Lad
Of small regard to see to, yet well skill'd
In every vertuous plant and healing herb 620

86

That spreds her verdant leaf to th'morning ray,
He lov'd me well, and oft would beg me sing,
Which when I did, he on the tender grass
Would sit, and hearken even to extasie,
And in requital ope his leathern scrip,
And shew me simples of a thousand names
Telling their strange and vigorous faculties;
Amongst the rest a small unsightly root,
But of divine effect, he cull'd me out;
The leaf was darkish, and had prickles on it,   630
But in another Countrey, as he said,
Bore a bright golden flowre, but not in this soyl:
Unknown, and like esteem'd, and the dull swayn
Treads on it daily with his clouted shoon,
And yet more med'cinal is it then that *Moly*
That *Hermes* once to wise *Ulysses* gave;
He call'd it *Hæmony*, and gave it me,
And bad me keep it as of sov'ran use
'Gainst all inchantments, mildew blast, or damp
Or gastly furies apparition;   640
I purs't it up, but little reck'ning made,
Till now that this extremity compell'd,
But now I find it true; for by this means
I knew the foul inchanter though disguis'd,
Enter'd the very lime-twigs of his spells,
And yet came off: if you have this about you
(As I will give you when we go) you may
Boldly assault the necromancers hall;
Where if he be, with dauntless hardihood,
And brandish't blade rush on him, break his glass   650
And shed the lushious liquor on the ground,
But sease his wand, though he and his curst crew
Feirce signe of battail make, and menace high,
Or like the sons of *Vulcan* vomit smoak,
Yet will they soon retire, if he but shrink.

Eld. Bro. *Thyrsis* lead on apace, Ile follow thee,
And som good angel bear a shield before us.

*The Scene changes to a stately Palace, set out with all manner of deliciousness:
soft Musick, Tables spred with all dainties.* Comus *appears with his rabble,
and the Lady set in an inchanted Chair, to whom he offers his Glass, which
she puts by, and goes about to rise.*

   Comus. Nay Lady sit; if I but wave this wand,
Your nerves are all chain'd up in Alablaster,
And you a statue, or as *Daphne* was   660
Root-bound, that fled *Apollo*.
   La. Fool do not boast,
Thou canst not touch the freedom of my minde
With all thy charms, although this corporal rinde
Thou haste immanacl'd, while Heav'n sees good.
   Co. Why are you vext Lady? why do you frown?
Here dwell no frowns, nor anger, from these gates
Sorrow flies far: See here be all the pleasures
That fancy can beget on youthfull thoughts,
When the fresh blood grows lively, and returns
Brisk as the *April* buds in Primrose-season.   670
And first behold this cordial Julep here
That flames, and dances in his crystal bounds
With spirits of balm, and fragrant Syrops mixt.
Not that *Nepenthes* which the wife of *Thone*,
In *Egypt* gave to *Jove*-born *Helena*
Is of such power to stir up joy as this,
To life so friendly, or so cool to thirst.
Why should you be so cruel to your self,
And to those dainty limms which nature lent
For gentle usage, and soft delicacy?   680
But you invert the cov'nants of her trust,
And harshly deal like an ill borrower
With that which you receiv'd on other terms,
Scorning the unexempt condition

88

By which all mortal frailty must subsist,
Refreshment after toil, ease after pain,
That have been tir'd all day without repast,
And timely rest have wanted, but fair Virgin
This will restore all soon.

    La. 'Twill not false traitor,
'Twill not restore the truth and honesty   690
That thou hast banish't from thy tongue with lies,
Was this the cottage, and the safe abode
Thou told'st me of? What grim aspects are these,
These oughly-headed Monsters? Mercy guard me!
Hence with thy brew'd inchantments, foul deceiver,
Hast thou betrai'd my credulous innocence
With visor'd falshood, and base forgery,
And wouldst thou seek again to trap me here
With lickerish baits fit to ensnare a brute?
Were it a draft for *Juno* when she banquets,   700
I would not taste thy treasonous offer; none
But such as are good men can give good things,
And that which is not good, is not delicious
To a wel-govern'd and wise appetite.

    Co. O foolishnes of men! that lend their ears
To those budge doctors of the *Stoick* Furr,
And fetch their precepts from the *Cynick* Tub,
Praising the lean and sallow Abstinence.
Wherefore did Nature powre her bounties forth,
With such a full and unwithdrawing hand,   710
Covering the earth with odours, fruits, and flocks,
Thronging the Seas with spawn innumerable,
But all to please, and sate the curious taste?
And set to work millions of spinning Worms,
That in their green shops weave the smooth-hair'd silk
To deck her Sons, and that no corner might
Be vacant of her plenty, in her own loyns
She hutch't th'all-worshipt ore, and precious gems

To store her children with; if all the world
Should in a pet of temperance feed on Pulse,   720
Drink the clear stream, and nothing wear but Freize,
Th'all-giver would be unthank't, would be unprais'd,
Not half his riches known, and yet despis'd,
And we should serve him as a grudging master,
As a penurious niggard of his wealth,
And live like Natures bastards, not her sons,
Who would be quite surcharg'd with her own weight,
And strangl'd with her waste fertility;
Th'earth cumber'd, and the wing'd air dark't with plumes,
The herds would over-multitude their Lords,   730
The Sea o'refraught would swell, & th'unsought diamonds
Would so emblaze the forhead of the Deep,
And so bestudd with Stars, that they below
Would grow inur'd to light, and com at last
To gaze upon the Sun with shameles brows.
List Lady be not coy, and be not cosen'd
With that same vaunted name Virginity,
Beauty is natures coyn, must not be hoorded,
But must be currant, and the good thereof
Consists in mutual and partak'n bliss,   740
Unsavoury in th'injoyment of it self
If you let slip time, like a neglected rose
It withers on the stalk with languish't head.
Beauty is natures brag, and must be shown
In courts, at feasts, and high solemnities
Where most may wonder at the workmanship;
It is for homely features to keep home,
They had their name thence; course complexions
And cheeks of sorry grain will serve to ply
The sampler, and to teize the huswifes wooll.   750
What need a vermeil-tinctur'd lip for that
Love-darting eyes, or tresses like the Morn?
There was another meaning in these gifts,

Think what, and be adviz'd, you are but young yet.

   La. I had not thought to have unlockt my lips
In this unhallow'd air, but that this Jugler
Would think to charm my judgement, as mine eyes
Obtruding false rules pranckt in reasons garb.
I hate when vice can bolt her arguments,
And vertue has no tongue to check her pride: 760
Impostor do not charge most innocent nature,
As if she would her children should be riotous
With her abundance she good cateres
Means her provision only to the good
That live according to her sober laws,
And holy dictate of spare Temperance:
If every just man that now pines with want
Had but a moderate and beseeming share
Of that which lewdly-pamper'd Luxury
Now heaps upon som few with vast excess,   770
Natures full blessings would be well dispenc't
In unsuperfluous eeven proportion,
And she no whit encomber'd with her store,
And then the giver would be better thank't,
His praise due paid, for swinish gluttony
Ne're looks to Heav'n amidst his gorgeous feast,
But with besotted base ingratitude
Cramms, and blasphemes his feeder. Shall I go on?
Or have I said anow? To him that dares
Arm his profane tongue with contemptuous words   780
Against the Sun-clad power of Chastity;
Fain would I somthing say, yet to what end?
Thou hast nor Ear, nor Soul to apprehend
The sublime notion, and high mystery
That must be utter'd to unfold the sage
And serious doctrine of Virginity,
And thou art worthy that thou shouldst not know
More happiness then this thy present lot.

Enjoy your dear Wit, and gay Rhetorick   790
That hath so well been taught her dazling fence,
Thou art not fit to hear thy self convinc't;
Yet should I try, the uncontrouled worth
Of this pure cause would kindle my rap't spirits
To such a flame of sacred vehemence,
That dumb things would be mov'd to sympathize,
And the brute Earth would lend her nerves, and shake,
Till all thy magick structures rear'd so high,
Where shatter'd into heaps o're thy false head.
   Co. She fables not, I feel that I do fear
Her words set off by som superior power;   800
And though not mortal, yet a cold shuddring dew
Dips me all o're, as when the wrath of *Jove*
Speaks thunder, and the chains of *Erebus*
To som of *Saturns* crew. I must dissemble,
And try her yet more strongly. Com, no more,
This is meer moral babble, and direct
Against the canon laws of our foundation;
I must not suffer this, yet 'tis but the lees
And setlings of a melancholy blood;
But this will cure all streight, one sip of this   810
Will bathe the drooping spirits in delight
Beyond the bliss of dreams. Be wise, and taste.—

The Brothers rush in with Swords drawn, wrest his Glass out of his hand, and break it against the ground; his rout make sign of resistance, but are all driven in; The attendant Spirit comes in.

   Spir. What, have you let the false Enchanter scape?
O ye mistook, ye should have snatcht his wand
And bound him fast; without his rod revers't,
And backward mutters of dissevering power,
We cannot free the Lady that sits here
In stony fetters fixt, and motionless;
Yet stay, be not disturb'd, now I bethink me,

Som other means I have which may be us'd,   820
Which once of *Melibœus* old I learnt
The soothest Shepherd that ere pip't on plains.
    There is a gentle Nymph not far from hence,
That with moist curb sways the smooth Severn stream,
Sabrina is her name, a Virgin pure,
Whilom she was the daughter of *Locrine*,
That had the Scepter from his Father *Brute*.
The guiltless damsel flying the mad pursuit
Of her enraged stepdam *Guendolen*,
Commended her fair innocence to the flood   830
That stay'd her flight with his cross-flowing course,
The water Nymphs that in the bottom plaid,
Held up their pearled wrists and took her in,
Bearing her straight to aged *Nereus* Hall,
Who piteous of her woes, rear'd her lank head,
And gave her to his daughters to imbathe
In nectar'd lavers strew'd with Asphodil,
And through the porch and inlet of each sense
Dropt in Ambrosial Oils till she reviv'd,
And underwent a quick immortal change   840
Made Goddess of the River; still she retains
Her maid'n gentlenes, and oft at Eeve
Visits the herds along the twilight meadows,
Helping all urchin blasts, and ill luck signes
That the shrewd medling Elfe delights to make,
Which she with pretious viold liquors heals.
For which the Shepherds at their festivals
Carrol her goodnes lowd in rustick layes,
And throw sweet garland wreaths into her stream
Of pancies, pinks, and gaudy Daffadils.   850
And, as the old Swain said, she can unlock
The clasping charm, and thaw the numming spell,
If she be right invok't in warbled Song,
For maid'nhood she loves, and will be swift

To aid a Virgin, such as was her self
In hard besetting need, this will I try
And adde the power of som adjuring verse.

SONG.

Sabrina fair
    Listen where thou art sitting
      Under the glassie, cool, translucent wave,   860
      In twisted braids of Lillies knitting
    The loose train of thy amber-dropping hair,
      Listen for dear honours sake,
      Goddess of the silver lake,
              Listen and save.

Listen and appear to us
In name of great *Oceanus,*
By the earth-shaking *Neptune*'s mace,
And *Tethys* grave majestick pace,
By hoary *Nereus* wrincled look,   870
And the *Carpathian* wisards hook,
By scaly *Tritons* winding shell,
And old sooth-saying *Glaucus* spell,
By *Leucothea*'s lovely hands,
And her son that rules the strands,
By *Thetis* tinsel-slipper'd feet,
And the Songs of *Sirens* sweet,
By dead *Parthenope*'s dear tomb,
And fair *Ligea*'s golden comb,
Wherwith she sits on diamond rocks   880
Sleeking her soft alluring locks,
By all the *Nymphs* that nightly dance
Upon thy streams with wily glance,
Rise, rise, and heave thy rosie head
From thy coral-pav'n bed,

94

And bridle in thy headlong wave,
Till thou our summons answerd have.

Listen and save.

Sabrina *rises, attended by water-Nymphs, sings.*

By the rushy-fringed bank,
Where grows the Willow and the Osier dank,   890
   My sliding Chariot stayes,
Thick set with Agat, and the azurn sheen
  Of Turkis blew, and Emrauld green
     That in the channel strayes,
    Whilst from off the waters fleet
    Thus I set my printless feet
   O're the Cowslips Velvet head,
    That bends not as I tread,
   Gentle swain at thy request
    I am here.   900

Spir. Goddess dear
We implore thy powerful hand
To undoe the charmed band
Of true Virgin here distrest,
Through the force, and through the wile
Of unblest inchanter vile.
Sab. Shepherd 'tis my office best
To help insnared chastity;
Brightest Lady look on me,
Thus I sprinkle on thy brest   910
Drops that from my fountain pure,
I have kept of pretious cure,
Thrice upon thy fingers tip,
Thrice upon thy rubied lip,
Next this marble venom'd seat
Smear'd with gumms of glutenous heat
I touch with chaste palms moist and cold,

95

Now the spell hath lost his hold;
And I must haste ere morning hour
To wait in *Amphitrite*'s bowr.   920

    Sabrina descends, and the Lady rises out of her seat.

  Spir. Virgin, daughter of *Locrine*
Sprung of old *Anchises* line,
May thy brimmed waves for this
Their full tribute never miss
From a thousand petty rills,
That tumble down the snowy hills:
Summer drouth, or singed air
Never scorch thy tresses fair,
Nor wet *Octobers* torrent flood
Thy molten crystal fill with mudd,   930
May thy billows rowl ashoar
The beryl, and the golden ore,
May thy lofty head be crown'd
With many a tower and terras round,
And here and there thy banks upon
With Groves of myrrhe, and cinnamon.
Com Lady while Heaven lends us grace,
Let us fly this cursed place,
Lest the Sorcerer us entice
With som other new device.   940
Not a waste, or needless sound
Till we com to holier ground,
I shall be your faithfull guide
Through this gloomy covert wide,
And not many furlongs thence
Is your Fathers residence,
Where this night are met in state
Many a friend to gratulate
His wish't presence, and beside
All the Swains that there abide,   950

96

With Jiggs, and rural dance resort,
We shall catch them at their sport,
And our sudden coming there
Will double all their mirth and chere;
Com let us haste, the Stars grow high,
But night sits monarch yet in the mid sky.

The Scene changes, presenting Ludlow *Town and the Presidents Castle, then
  com in Countrey-Dancers, after them the attendant Spirit, with the two
  Brothers and the Lady.*

SONG.

   Spir. *Back Shepherds, back, anough your play,*
Till next Sun-shine holiday,
Here be without duck or nod
Other trippings to be trod   960
Of lighter toes, and such Court guise
As Mercury *did first devise*
With the mincing Dryades
On the Lawns, and on the Leas.

      This second Song presents them to their Father and Mother.

Noble Lord, and Lady bright,
I have brought ye new delight,
Here behold so goodly grown
Three fair branches of your own,
Heav'n hath timely tri'd their youth,
Their faith, their patience, and their truth.   970
And sent them here through hard assays
With a crown of deathless Praise,
   To triumph in victorious dance
O're sensual Folly, and Intemperance.

        The dances ended, the Spirit Epiloguizes.

Spir. To the Ocean now I fly,
And those happy climes that ly
Where day never shuts his eye,
Up in the broad fields of the sky:
There I suck the liquid air
All amidst the Gardens fair   980
Of *Hesperus*, and his daughters three
That sing about the golden tree:
Along the crisped shades and bowres
Revels the spruce and jocond Spring,
The Graces, and the rosie-boosom'd Howres,
Thither all their bounties bring,
That there eternal Summer dwels,
And West winds, with musky wing
About the cedar'n alleys fling
Nard, and *Cassia*'s balmy smels.   990
Iris there with humid bow,
Waters the odorous banks that blow
Flowers of more mingled hew
Then her purfl'd scarf can shew,
And drenches with *Elysian* dew
(List mortals if your ears be true)
Beds of *Hyacinth*, and Roses
Where young *Adonis* oft reposes,
Waxing well of his deep wound
In slumber soft, and on the ground   1000
Sadly sits th' *Assyrian* Queen;
But far above in spangled sheen
Celestial *Cupid* her fam'd Son advanc't,
Holds his dear *Psyche* sweet intranc't
After her wandring labours long,
Till free consent the gods among
Make her his eternal Bride,
And from her fair unspotted side
Two blissful twins are to be born,

Youth and Joy; so *Jove* hath sworn. 1010
   But now my task is smoothly don,
I can fly, or I can run
Quickly to the green earths end,
Where the bow'd welkin slow doth bend,
And from thence can soar as soon
To the corners of the Moon.
   Mortals that would follow me,
Love vertue, she alone is free,
She can teach ye how to clime
Higher then the Spheary chime; 1020
Or if Vertue feeble were,
Heav'n it self would stoop to her.
[1645]
[1673 then has verse paraphrases of Psalms 1–8 (1653) and **Psalms 80–88**
   (1648) which are omitted from this edition.]

COMMENTARY AND NOTES

7. THE STATIONER TO THE READER

The Stationer: publisher. The claim which Moseley makes for his record as a publisher is quite justified: he published instructive prose works and poetry. Besides Milton he published Waller, Crashaw, Shirley, Suckling, and Cowley.

*l.*10. *Sir Henry Wootton:* (1568–1639) diplomat and poet. He had been ambassador in Venice for much of the time between 1604 and 1624 and was appointed Provost of Eton in 1624. Milton had visited him at Eton, and he had given Milton advice and addresses for his trip to Europe in 1638. Milton had sent him a copy of the 1637 edition of *Comus,* and a letter from Wootton acknowledging this and praising the poem was included in the 1645 edition of the poems (see introductory note to *Comus*).

*l.*11. *dainties:* estimable, choice things.

*l.*15. *Waller:* Edmund Waller (1606–87), M.P. and poet. Politically a moderate, he was drawn increasingly to the King's side in the Civil War and was involved in 1643 in a plot to seize London for Charles. The plot was discovered and he was heavily fined and banished. He remained in exile until he was pardoned in 1651. It is interesting that Waller's political activities did not prejudice the publication of his poems in 1645. As with many of Milton's poems in this volume, poetry sets itself apart from politics.

*l.*21. *Spencer:* Edmund Spenser (1552–99) was a key figure in the establishment of the English poetic tradition, especially through his works in the pastoral (*The Shepheardes Calender*) and heroic (*The Faerie Queene*) genres. His type of poetry—moral, courtly, and 'poetical' in style and diction—was deeply influential, and Moseley's associating Milton's poetry with it is very significant and proper.

POEMS

8. ON THE MORNING OF CHRISTS NATIVITY

Written in 1629, this is not the earliest of Milton's English poems: the 1645 edition included the paraphrases of Psalms 114 and 136 which were both written in 1623 and the 1673 edition added the earlier *Death of a Fair Infant etc.* and *At A Vacation Exercise.* But Milton may have had some point in putting this poem first since of all his minor poems it most fully presents his personality and his interests. In the other major poems in this volume Milton, appropriately enough indulging and demonstrating his learning and elegance, does not write in a fully Christian vein, but this poem has an explicit Christian theme as its subject and is concerned with the dismissal of the classical and pagan world. It thus importantly demonstrates his religious intensity and his intellectual power and is the truest precursor of *Paradise Lost* and the later poems. It does not surprise us to find that the writer of this poem was also to become the controvertist and the historian. His Christ child is typically more the forerunner of that aggressive Christ who drove the moneylenders from the temple than of the Christ who suffered the little children to come to Him. All this affects the way in which Milton presents the Nativity. He recognizes the meanness of the stable (*l.*31) only to see it as transformed into a court by the royal presence of the world's King (*l.*243), of whose power the kings of the world stand hushed in awe (*l.*59) and whose coming humiliated the pagan gods. That Christ Himself was threatened by a powerful enemy in King Herod is suitably enough omitted.

Like all of Milton's major work the poem has spaciousness and variety. Around the central picture of the child in the stable (*ll.*29–31; 152; 237–43) are woven elaborate digressions into space and time. The Nativity is presented not simply as an event in one single place at one single time but as an event in a process that extends through all history from the Creation to the Day of Judgement, and all of Creation is shown aware of Christ's presence. It has too a variety of manner being in turn sublime, satiric, lyrical and tender. But it remains always consciously poetical. It has a characteristic self-consciousness of manner, the four-stanza prelude to the hymn showing us Milton very aware of himself as the poet writing a poem. To mark the impressiveness of the occasion which he is celebrating and his own poetic virtuosity Milton uses an elaborate stanza form of his own invention which requires some skill to manage. He calls his poem an ode (*l.*24), a type of poem that was high and exalted in manner. There is wit and conceitedness—a tactic of clever and ingenious refinement and complication—in many of the episodes. The diction is formal and poetical, not familiar or colloquial. There is some archaising, but the device is not used very intensively. Much more noteworthy are the compound adjectives and a studied poeticism of diction (e.g. in words like *deadly, darksom, spangled, paramour, Harbinger, glimmering, bespake, shady, warbl'd, thrilling, weltring, chime, dolorous, sheen, tissu'd, smouldring, scaly, grisly, unshowr'd, sable, orient, polisht*). The poem's authority and assurance are remarkably precocious.

*l.*5. *holy Sages:* the Old Testament prophets who had foretold the coming of the Messiah.

*l.*6. *deadly forfeit:* the penalty of death imposed upon Man as the consequence of Adam's sinful disobedience.

*l.*15. *Heav'nly Muse:* the nine Muses were daughters of Zeus and were regarded as the inspirers of learning and the arts, especially poetry and music. Milton calls his Muse *Heav'nly* to stress the Christian inspiration of his poem.

*l.*19. *Suns team:* the depiction of the sun in its course as a charioteer derives from classical mythology (cf. *l.*84).

*l.*23. *Star-led Wisards:* the wise men from the East who followed the star to Bethlehem (Matthew 2). To call them *Wisards* emphasizes their skill in astrology.

*l.*24. *prevent:* arrive before.

*l.*28. A reference to Isaiah 6, where the prophet's lips are purified by being touched with a live coal which a seraph has taken from the altar of God. *Paradise Lost* also opens with the insistence on the need for the Christian poet to sing with a pure heart.

*ll.*37–52. An elaborate mythological invention of the type for which Ovid was the pattern. The trick is to provide mythological reasons for explaining why things are as they are. Thus, in *Metamorphoses*, IV, *ll.*740–52, Ovid explicates the fact that coral is a plant in water but a rock in air by supposing that it acquired this strange nature when the head of the Gorgon Medusa (which turned all that it gazed upon to stone) was buried by the shore and so communicated its own strange relation with softness and stone to certain plants in the sea. Here Milton is making the simple point that it did not snow in

Palestine even though it was midwinter (the shepherds and their flocks were after all out in the fields), but he rather mishandles it. Nature, he argues, would be glad of some snow in order to hide her shame, but Christ in His mercy sends down Peace crowned with green in order to assuage her fears. In so far as the conceit thus makes a point about the graciousness of Christ it is a success, but Milton gets into trouble with the way he presents Nature. He says she is ashamed and contrite before her Lord (*ll*.39–45) which is proper, but unfortunately suggests also that she is a coquette and a hypocrite in that those talents which she had before used to wanton with the sun (*l*.36) are now used to woo the air to hide what she is (*ll*.37–9).

l.47.   *Olive:* a conventional emblem of peace.

l.48.   *turning sphear:* the sphere of the heavens which turned daily about the earth. Milton throughout his early poems uses the old (classical and medieval) astronomy. Pythagoras (6th century B.C.) had first posited that the earth was a sphere and that the whole universe—the spheres of the seven planets and the fixed stars—rotated about an axis passing through its centre. His system presented some difficulties, especially in respect of the lack of uniformity in the motion of the planets, and it was consequently developed and refined. One of the most influential accounts is that of Plato (4th century B.C.) in *Republic*, Book X (see note on *Arcades*, *ll*.62–73). Eudoxus and Aristotle (both 4th century B.C.) developed the important theory that the universe consisted of a set of concentric spheres though they differed as to their number. It was Ptolemy (2nd century A.D.) who developed the system in the form which remained established until the 16th century. In this system the earth was the still centre of the universe. It was surrounded by nine spheres, firstly the spheres in which the seven planets (the Moon, Mercury, Venus, the Sun, Mars, Jupiter, and lastly Saturn) moved, then the eighth sphere containing the fixed stars, and lastly the outermost sphere (the *Primum Mobile*) which gave motion to all the others. The whole picture required some mathematical complexity in order to square it with what was observed about the sky and its motions. The Middle Ages continued to refine and adjust the system in the light of their increasing knowledge, but in the 16th and 17th centuries observation and mathematics combined (with Copernicus, Galileo, Brahe, Kepler, and finally Newton) to develop the new astronomy which replaced the old earth-centred universe by the modern sun-centred one in which the earth moved like the other planets. The clash between the two systems had important theological repercussions since the new astronomy contradicted the Bible which clearly envisaged a universe in which the sun moved round the earth (see Genesis 1: 16–17; Joshua 10: 12–13; Job 26: 7; Psalm 19: 4–6; Ps. 75: 3; Ps. 93: 1; Ps. 104: 5; Ps. 119:90; Jeremiah 10:12), and Galileo for example was forced by the church to retract his belief in the new system. How important the issue was can be seen in Marlowe's *Doctor Faustus* (circ.

1592) sc. vi, where Faustus in his pursuit of knowledge asks Mephistophilis for the truth about the motions of the stars and the number of the spheres.

Milton certainly knew about the new astronomy, although he did not of course know the form which the final solution took at the end of the 17th century. Adam's discussion with the archangel Raphael in *Paradise Lost*, VIII, is concerned with the dispute and its difficulties. However throughout his early poems he uses the old system whose poetical advantages are obvious since by placing the earth at the centre of the universe it usefully exemplified the importance of Man in the eyes of Heaven. Stripped of the mathematical complications that it actually required the old system presented a cosmos of beautiful simplicity and order.

The fact that astronomy was closely connected with mathematics also enabled Greek philosophers to connect it with music which was also concerned with ratio and proportion. Thus Pythagoras was led to develop his concept of the music of the spheres. The manner in which the sound of the notes upon a string varied with the length of the string was taken to exemplify the law which regulated the distance of the various planets from the earth. Astronomy and harmonics were thus conjoined, and each planet was held to sound a note of music, the whole producing a harmonious chord. Man was not aware of hearing this music since (as he had naturally heard it continuously from his birth) it made up a part of what he apprehended as silence. A neo-Platonic and Christian refinement of this unawareness was to suppose that it stemmed from the grossness which came with Man's loss of his original moral perfection. But this concept of the harmony of the spheres was not a necessary part of the old astronomy. Aristotle had regarded it as implausible, and Ptolemy had ignored it. We know that Milton disbelieved it as a matter of science since in an oration which he made in Cambridge as part of his university training (the *Second Prolusion*: 'On the Music of the Spheres') he argues that Pythagoras had developed the idea simply as a metaphorical representation of the order and harmony of the created world. It is in this way that he uses it himself in his poetry.

l.50.   *Turtle wing:* winged like the turtle dove which was emblematic of constant love. Cf. too the descent of the Holy Spirit as a dove at the baptism of Christ (Matthew 3: 16).

l.50.   *amorous clouds:* the clouds also are ardent with love of Peace.

l.51.   *mirtle:* the myrtle (sacred to Venus in Roman times) was emblematic of love.

ll.53–60.   In this stanza Milton is referring to the historical fact that the world was at peace when Christ was born. The reference to the Messiah in Isaiah 9: 6 as 'The Prince of Peace' was taken as prophetic of this.

l.56.   *hooked:* the wheels of the chariots were fitted with projecting sharp hooks to add to their destructive power when in motion.

l.64. *whist:* hushed.

l.68. *Birds of Calm:* halcyons (kingfishers) were anciently supposed to lay their eggs in midwinter in a nest upon the sea (hence *brooding*). They were supposed to cast a spell upon the waters (hence *charmed wave*) so that they remained calm during this period ('halcyon days'). But the coming of Christ casts a new spell upon the waters.

l.71. *influence:* an invisible fluid was held to *flow* downward from the stars and to exert a powerful force upon the destiny of men and things. It was often of a baleful sort but here is *precious* as suits this moment in history. The stars often opposed each other in their effects but here they shed their power in unison (*bending one way*). In *Paradise Lost*, before the Fall, the stars had shed 'sweet influence' (VII, 375): it was Man's sin that made them malign (X, 655–664).

l.74. *Lucifer:* the morning-star. No reference to Satan is intended here.

l.77. *gloom:* in its sense here: 'an indefinite degree of darkness' the word is a new poetical formation of Milton's own.

ll.85–92. Milton's presentation of the Biblical shepherds is coloured by his knowledge of classical pastoral poetry where shepherds are often enough lovers.

l.89. *mighty Pan*: Pan was the classical god of shepherds, often taken in Christian poetry of the Renaissance as the Creator or Christ Himself. Milton's use of the phrase here may however be sarcastic. The shepherds are about to be struck by wonder and surprise, and Milton marks this by using their terminology about an event (i.e. the Creator Himself becoming one of his creatures) which their ideology had never at all envisaged.

l.90. *kindly:* (i) 'in their own kind as man' and (ii) 'lovingly'.

l.92. *silly:* unlearned.

l.97. *stringed noise:* cf. *Harping* (*l.115*). The account in Luke 2 says nothing about harps, but Revelation 14: 2 shows that they accompanied angelic voices on great occasions.

l.100. *close:* a musical cadence.

ll.102–3. *the hollow round/Of Cynthia's seat:* a poetical phrase for the orbit of the moon (Cynthia or Artemis, the moon goddess, was supposed to have been born on Mt Cynthus in Delos) beneath which everything since the Fall of Man was subject to change. Above the moon's orbit was the world of perfection and constancy, but with Christ's birth Nature thinks that her kingdom on earth now shares that heavenly perfection.

l.116. *unexpressive:* inexpressible.

ll.117–32. It should be noticed how Milton develops the classical idea of the music of the spheres in a fully Christian way and with Biblical authority. The universe was established in stability and harmony, and the first song that was heard was that of the *sons of morning*. This singing is a combination of the two songs of praise which, according to Job 38: 8, celebrated the creation of the world: 'When the morning stars sang together, and all the sons of God [i.e. angels] shouted for joy'. At the Nativity the Bible says that the singing was done by a 'multitude of the heavenly host' (Luke 2: 13) and says nothing about the stars. But Milton takes this Biblical phrase in a wide sense to include all the heavens (i.e. stars as well as angels): if angels and stars sang together when the world was made, it was not unreasonable to suppose that they sang together when Christ was born. We cannot as Milton points out (*l.*127) hear the music of the spheres, but then we cannot hear the stars either, but Job says that they could sing. Milton almost certainly regarded the singing of the stars in Job as a metaphorical expression anyway, perfectly proper to the Scriptures and to God's way of making Himself and His ways known to His creatures.

*l.*122. *hinges:* the axes between the four cardinal points of the earth.

*l.*126. *humane:* i.e. human.

*l.*130. *the Base:* i.e. the earth itself since earth is the heaviest of the four elements of which the universe is made.

*l.*131. *ninefold harmony:* Milton like some earlier writers makes the ninth sphere sing (though it is unmoving) in order to match the spheres' song to that of the nine orders of angels. The Bible indicates that there are different orders of angels but does not specify nine. This number (developed especially in the writings of the Pseudo-Dionysius, circ. 5th century A.D.) reflects the systematic application to Biblical material of the same mystic sense of number (3×3) that had played a part in the concept of the music of the spheres.

*l.*135. *age of gold:* the first and finest age of the world when Man lived innocent and prosperous. But the world slowly degenerated through the ages of silver, bronze, and iron until finally man's wickedness drove Astraea, the goddess of justice, from the earth (cf. *ll.*141–2). A classical idea (see, for example, Ovid, Metamorphoses, I, 89–162) but one clearly capable of Christian application (as here) to the age of innocence in which Adam lived before his sin, and to the blissful life which redeemed Man will enjoy.

*ll.*143–4. Note the revision of these lines. Though some decorativeness is lost, the alteration increases the scriptural weight of the poem since it brings in an allusion to Revelation 10: 1 ('And I saw another mighty angel come down from heaven, clothed with a cloud, and a rainbow upon his head, and his face was as it were the sun, and his feet as pillars of fire') where the angel announces the Last Judgement—which is what Milton is describing here.

*l.*145. *sheen:* brightness. A poetical word.

*l.*146. *tissued:* a vivid metaphor. Tissue is a rich cloth often interwoven with gold or silver thread.

*l.*149. *wisest Fate:* note how Milton here christianizes a pagan idea. Fate is a blind power which compels men to their destiny, but by insisting here that it is *wisest Fate* that speaks Milton points to the intelligent and providential nature of the Christian God.

*l.*155. *ychain'd:* poetical use of an archaic past participle.

*ll.*157-64. According to Exodus 19: 16 Mount Sinai was disturbed with storm and cloud when Moses brought the Israelites into God's presence to recive the commandments, and Christ also prophesied (Matthew 24: 29) that His second coming would be heralded by darkness and disturbance in the heavens.

*l.*157. *clang:* loud sound, originally (as here) of a trumpet.

*l.*159. *smouldring:* suffocating. Poetical diction. During the 17th and 18th centuries this pres. part. was the only form of the verb in use, and was found only in poetry.

*l.*164. *in middle Air:* according to Revelation 20: 11, when Christ sets up His throne, the earth and heavens shall flee from His face, thus leaving nothing between Heaven and Hell but air.

*l.*172. *swindges:* thrashes about   *foulded:* coiled.

*ll.*173-236. Milton at length and with some force and sarcasm illustrates the way in which the pagan gods were crushed by the coming of the true God. In his careful and knowledgeable discrimination between the various forms of pagan worship we can see the historian and theologian in the poet. The Roman gods (*ll.*181-9) for example are presented in a graceful elegiac tone whereas the Egyptian gods are presented with a harshness that suits their brutality. We do not have to go on to suppose from this that Milton regrets the passing of these Roman figures. The Roman mythology is certainly more creditable than the Egyptian, but Christ's coming has made a choice between them unnecessary.

*l.*174. *The oracles are dum:* a fine ironic touch. The oracles deceive in their speaking (*l.*175) but their silence here is equally discreditable. When the most important event in human history occurred, the oracles failed to foretell it.

*l.*176. *Apollo:* the classical god of music and prophecy whose most important shrine was at Delphi. Notice how here, where questions of belief are very relevant, Milton's attitude to classical mythology is hostile and critical. (Contrast the less ideological but more poetical reference to Cynthia earlier (*l.*103)).

*l.*186. *Genius:* in Roman mythology the guardian deity of a place.

*l.*188. Mourning was a characteristic exercise of nymphs in classical pastoral elegy. Milton is perhaps sarcastically implying that this time they had something really important to shed tears about viz. their own supersession.

*l.*191. *Lars* were the ghosts of the dead and were honoured and propitiated at ritual places and in the home itself. *Lemures* were ghosts without kin who were supposed to haunt households on various days.

*l.*193. *drear:* doleful (a poetical form of 'dreary').

*l.*194. *Flamins:* ritual priests of the Roman gods.

*l.*195. The condensation of moisture upon marble made for this sort of conceited application. Cf. Ovid's account (*Metamorphoses* VI: 301–12) of Niobe's weeping even though she is turned to stone. Virgil in *Georgics* I: 480, describes how bronze statues sweated with fear as an omen of Caesar's assassination.

*l.*196. *peculiar:* i.e. having its own especial jurisdiction.

*l.*197. *Peor:* Moabite god of uncleanness.

*l.*197. *Baalim:* chief male deity of the Phoenicians and Canaanites for whom on occasion (e.g. Judges 2: 11) the Israelites forsook their God.

*l.*199. i.e. Dagon, national god of the Philistines. In 1 Samuel 5 the ark of God is twice set before the statue of Dagon, and the statue is twice found fallen upon its face before the ark.

*l.*200. *mooned Ashtaroth:* chief female deity (hence *Heav'ns . . . Mother*) of the Phoenicians and Canaanites who (like Baal) was sometimes impiously worshipped by the Israelites (e.g. Judges 2: 13). She was identified with the Syrian Astarte and Greek Aphrodite. Her image was the moon (as Baal's was the sun). She is called 'the queen of heaven' in Jeremiah 7: 18.

*l.*203. The most frequent representation of the Libyan god Hammon was as a woolly ram with curved horns. Hence Milton's contemptuous *shrinks his horn* as a sign of his lost power. The phrase is usually used of a snail drawing in its horns so Milton's application of it to a ram is deliberately scornful.

*l.*204. *Thamuz:* a Syrian and Phoenician god, the son of Ashtaroth, and associated with the Greek Adonis. Women weep for him in Ezekiel 8: 14.

*l.*205. *Moloch:* god of the Ammonites whose worship is associated with fire (e.g. Leviticus 18: 21). Hence *sullen* here means 'dark' as well as 'downcast': Moloch's fire is quenched by the power of Christ.

*l.*211. According to Plutarch, *De Isis et Osiris*, from whom Milton derived much of the material in these verses, Egyptian worship differed significantly from the Greek in that whereas the latter held certain animals to be sacred to certain gods (e.g. the dove to Aphrodite), the former reverenced the animals themselves as gods. Hence Milton emphasizes throughout this section the animal nature of the Egyptian deities. *Isis* and *Osiris* were the chief Egyptian deities. Osiris who was worshipped in the bull (*l.*215) was murdered by his brother *Typhon*. *Orus*, a son of Osiris, helped Isis to avenge Osiris's death by putting Typhon to death. Typhon was regarded as the cause of evils and was worshipped in the crocodile, hence *ending in snaky twine* (*l.*226). *Anubis*, the son or brother of Osiris, was represented as having a dog's head.

*l.*215. *unshowr'd:* without rain.

*l.*219. *Timbrel'd:* accompanied by timbrels or tambourines.

*l.*223. *eyn:* a poetical archaism.

*ll.*229–36. A very logical stanza. Milton wishes to illustrate the idea in *ll.*227–8 of Christ controlling the heathen gods even though He is still a baby. He thus needs an image of power exerted with apparent effortlessness and from a supine position. *In bed* is thus logically necessary to show that the sun is powerful in precisely this way since ghosts disappear with the first glimpse of light, i.e. before he has got up. *In bed* is thus parallel to *in his swadling bands.* To indicate that the idea of the sun being in bed is not all that peculiar Milton adds *curtained* and *pillows* to show that the sun in the sky at dawn can properly be seen as a person in a bed. Milton's difficulty is that the sun's bed, with its apparent splendour of curtains and pillows, is very different from Christ's humble bed in a stable so that the two ideas fight as well as help each other.

*ll.*231–4. Ghosts and the spirits of the dead were popularly supposed to return to Hell or to their graves at the first glimmer of dawn.

*l.*234. *fetter'd:* i.e. unable to escape into the world of the spirit (cf. *Comus ll.* 469–75).

*l.*235. *Fays:* supernatural beings supposed to influence the affairs of men. Milton gives them a fairy attractiveness but they are sinister beings nonetheless.

*ll.*240–4. The poem closed on a deliberately elevated and richly poetical note.

*l.*240. *youngest teemed:* latest born i.e. the star of Bethlehem.

*l.*241. *polisht Car:* shining chariot. A very poetical expression.

*l.*244. *Bright-harnest:* clad in bright armour.

*l.*244. *serviceable:* ready to serve their Lord.

17. PSALM 136

Since the Psalms are songs—'a divine poem' according to Sir Philip Sidney—it was natural that poets should want to put them into metre, and this metrical paraphrasing was a common poetic exercise in the 16th and and 17th centuries. *Paraphrase* was a free (usually fuller and clearer) rendering: that it is in general longer than the original is not against the principles of the genre. This one of Milton's paraphrases is included in this edition to provide an example of a literary form that much exercised Milton. (In all, he paraphrased 19 psalms.) This particular one is still popular as a hymn of praise. Milton's use of very characteristic poetical effects should be noted especially the poetic diction (e.g. *painted, spangl'd, ruddy, warble* etc.) and compound adjectives. The style is influenced by Joshua Sylvester's translation (1605–8) of *His Deuine Weekes and Workes,* a long poetical and moralistic narrative poem on the Creation and Old Testament history by the French poet Du Bartas (1544–90), a poem very popular in the late 16th and 17th centuries. Reference to the psalm will clarify many of the details and will show that Milton has expanded his poem with details taken from other parts of the Old Testament. The psalm praises God for his creation of the world (*ll.*17–36), for his deliverance of the Israelites from bondage in Egypt (*ll.*37–56), with God's gift to them of the Promised Land (*ll.*57–76), and with God's loving kindness (*ll.*77–96).

l.46. *the Erythræan main:* the Red Sea, called Erythræan either because Erythras, son of Perseus and Andromeda, was drowned there, or because of the redness of its water.

l.54. *Tawny:* i.e. of a light brown (African) complexion.

l.61–76. Sihon, king of the Amorites, and Og, king of Bashan, opposed the Israelites on their journey out of the wilderness. They were both defeated in battle and the Israelites took their land (Numbers 21; Deuteronomy 2 and 3).

20. ON THE DEATH OF A FAIR INFANT DYING OF A COUGH

Though written, according to Milton's note, when he was 17 years of age, this poem was not included in the 1645 edition and was first published in 1673. It is much more obviously Spenserian than the *Nativity Ode*, and should be compared with Spenser's *Astrophel*, an elegy for Sir Philip Sidney. Its manner is ingeniously mythological and elaborate, with its compound adjectives, its poetical diction (e.g. *envermeil, bewayl'd, behoofe, reinstall, sheenie*) and its archaism (*eld, whilome, wight, weed*). Some of its paradoxes (e.g. *kiss/But kill'd; cold-kind*) are rather obvious, and, considering its subject, much of the treatment is rather tasteless.

Title: Cough: a lung disease such as bronchitis.

l.2. *timeleslie:* out of due time i.e. while still very young.

ll.8–21. A complicated mythological invention to explain the early death of the child in the winter of the year.

ll.8–21. *Aquilo* (Gk Boreas) was the god of the North Wind whose rape of the Athenian princess Orithyia is described in Ovid, *Metamorphoses*, VI, 682–713. Ovid in *Fasti*, V, 201–6 says that Boreas's rape of Orithyia gave his brother Zephyrus the idea of carrying off Flora. This may have encouraged Milton to develop his idea that Winter was incited by Boreas's success to carry off the child as his prize.

ll.23–8. Apollo loved the Laconian boy Hyacinth but accidentally killed him while competing with him in throwing the discus (see Ovid, *Metamorphoses*, X, 162–219).

l.25. *Eurota:* a river in Laconia.

l.31. *wormie bed:* cf. Shakespeare, *MND*, III, ii, 384.

l.39. *that high first-moving Spheare:* the *Primum Mobile* (see *Nativity Ode,* *l.*48 note. Beyond the *Primum Mobile* is Heaven, the dwelling of the blest.

l.40. *th'Elisian fields:* where, according to classical mythology, the souls of the virtuous went after death. Milton's doubt about them (*if such there were*) seems to indicate a sudden refusal of his Christian piety to keep up the mythological pretence which the poem has so far indulged.

ll.42–63. Milton invents a set of mythological episodes to account for the presence of an immortal upon earth.

l.44. *shak't Olympus:* Olympus, the home of the gods, was shaken when Jove hurled the Titans from Heaven.

l.45. *behoofe:* advantage.

ll.47–52. In the age of iron the earth became the prey of violence and crime. The giants of earth even attacked the heavens, but they were destroyed by Jove. This was the time when the last immortal, Astraea (Justice), left the earth (cf. *Nativity Ode, l.*135 note).

l.48. *sheenie:* bright. The adjective appears to be Milton's own poetical formation from the noun *sheen.*

l.53. The line lacks two syllables. It has been reasonably enough suggested that it should read: *Or wert thou Mercy that sweet smiling Youth?* since Truth, Justice, and Mercy are associated with each other in the *Nativity Ode, ll.*141–144, and Justice and Truth are mentioned here.

l.68. *slaughtering pestilence:* the plague. Milton makes a very topical application of his prayer.

ll.71–7. It should be noticed that this last stanza drops entirely the poetical, mythological manner and instead, in a simple and dignified way, presents the Christian consolation that Milton could, without qualification, associate himself with.

l.76. Cf. the consolation for the childless in Isaiah 56: 5: 'Even unto them will I give in my house and without my walls a name better than sons and of daughters: I will give them an everlasting name, that shall not be cut off'.

23. AT A VACATION EXERCISE IN THE COLLEDGE, ETC.

Like the preceding poem these lines were first published in the 1673 edition. According to Milton's headnote about his age they were written in the Long Vacation of 1628. The occasion was a type of college high jinks which took place at the end of the academic year in the presence of most of the teaching and student body. Milton must have made some mark academically to be asked to take so prominent a part in the affair. He had to make the chief speech and to introduce the other students who were taking part. The first part was in Latin and consisted of an oration on the appropriate theme that festivities are not always the enemy of academic study. This was followed by a prolusion (also in Latin) or literary exercise which developed the same theme in a more extravagantly fanciful and rumbustious manner. These Latin sections of the proceedings were published (*Prolusion VI*) with Milton's other academic exercises in 1674. Then followed these lines in English verse which served to introduce a sort of philosophical tableau on Aristotelian logic with Milton as Ens, the Father of Aristotle's categories, introducing his children. Like the Latin this English section is full of learned and private allusions, and Milton jokes at his audience's and his own expense. In the light of this we must not take what Milton says about himself and poetry too seriously. Read out of context, *ll*.29–52 can be made to sound like a very solemn commitment to poetry on Milton's part. He may well have made such a commitment, but the way he makes it here is all of a piece with the way in which he pitches his style a bit high (and sometimes low) to suit the occasion.

l.8. latter task: the earlier part had been in Latin.

l.18. wardrope: a room in which clothes were kept.

l.20. our late fantasticks: it is impossible to say what poetic school Milton is criticizing. *Late* could mean either 'recent but now outmoded and dead' or 'modern'. It is possible that Milton is referring to the school of metaphysical poetry, even though the style of this piece with its somewhat boisterous use of the heroic couplet itself owes something to the school of Donne. Herbert's poem 'Jordan (I)' shows that it was possible to use the techniques of metaphysical poetry even when attacking metaphysical poetry. On the other hand Milton may just as likely be referring to some private issue, or debate about poetry which would be familiar to his audience.

l.27. suspect: suspicion.

ll.33–52. Milton presents a series of vivid pictures of the ecstacy, power, and wisdom that belong to poets.

ll.35–9. His first picture is of *Apollo*, the god of music, entertaining the gods in Heaven. Classical accounts of Apollo represent him as *unshorn* in order to emphasize his youth, a point appropriately emphasized on this college occasion. The *thunderous throne* is that of Zeus. References to Zeus's power being in the thunder are common in Homer. *Hebe*, the daughter of Zeus and Hera, was the cupbearer of the gods. *Nectar* is the drink of the gods. Though built up out of familiar enough material (see especially the Homeric *Hymn to Apollo*) the picture as a whole seems to be Milton's own.

l.40. Spherse of watchful fire: i.e. the stars. Cf. *Nativity Ode, ll.* 21, 70.

l.42. lofts: attics. That they contain piles of thunder is witty.

*l.*43   *green-ey'd Neptune:* Neptune was the god of the sea and islands who
shared the universe with his brothers Jupiter (who held Heaven and Earth)
and Pluto (who held the underworld). That he is *green-ey'd* and *raves* applies
not merely in that he is the sea (he is commonly called the 'shaker of earth'
in Homer) but also in that he jealously quarrelled (*green* being the colour of
jealousy) with his brother Jupiter on the grounds that he had a lesser kingdom.

l.46.   Beldam: aged woman. Again witty as applied to Nature.

*ll.*48–50.   *Demodocus* was the minstrel of King Alcinous of Phaeacia who
entertained the court during Ulysses' stay there with the story of the Trojan
heroes (Homer, *Odyssey*, VIII). Ulysses weeps at his song because it tells the
story of his own grievous battles.

l.56.   thy Predicament: a pun: (i) an Aristotelian category, the subject of the
representation; (ii) the problem which Milton is having to face.

l.59.   Canons: (i) laws of logic; (ii) clergy (here the nine students) who with
the Dean (here *Ens*) at their head, govern a cathedral (here the college). Some
parody of a church ceremony may be intended.

*ll.*59–90.   A witty representation of the nature of Aristotle's categories. Sub-
stance (*Ens*), i.e. a particular man or thing, is the primary category (*l.75*),
but it can be apprehended only through the things that can be predicated
about it (*ll.*65–82). These are the nine secondary characteristics—quantity,
quality, relation, place, time, position, condition, action, passivity—or
accidents (*l.74*). Substance is characterized by the fact that it has no opposite
i.e. a thing cannot be both black and white (*ll.*83–5), yet it is capable of
admitting contrary qualities i.e. a thing can be black at one time and white at
another (*ll.*85–8).

l.90.   Gordian knot: Gordius, king of Phrygia, tied a difficult knot about which
the oracle prophecied that whosoever untied it should rule Asia. It was cut
by Alexander the Great. The phrase is used of a situation of incredible
difficulty dramatically solved.

*ll.*91–100.   *Ens's* address to a student named Rivers provided Milton with
the opportunity to present a poetic and no doubt partly jocular list of English
rivers. This topographical poetry is in the tradition of Spenser (see especially
The Faerie Queene, IV, XI on the marriage of the Thames and the Medway)
and Drayton (*Polyolbion*). Milton takes most of his details from them but adds
one or two touches of his own.

l.91.   utmost Tweed: i.e. England's most northerly river (see *FQ*, IV, XI,
xxxvi).

*ll.*91–100.   *gulphie Dun:* the river Don in the West Riding which is full of
eddies (*Polyolbion*, XXVIII, 35, 47).

l.94.   His thirty Armes: the thirty tributaries of the Trent. There is a punning
link between *thirty* and *Trent* (*FQ*, IV, XI, xxxv; *Polybn*, XXVI, 171; 187–
192).

l.95. *sullen Mole:* dark, because the river runs for three miles underground (*FQ*, IV, XI, xxxii; *Polybn*, XVII, 59–64).

l.96. refers to the story of Sabrina, the illegitimate daughter of Locrine, King of Britain, who with her mother was cast into the Severn by Gwendolen, Locrine's queen. Cf. *Comus*, 826–32 (*FQ*, II, X, xix; *Polybn*, VI, 130–78).

l.97. *Rockie Avon:* cf. *FQ*, IV, XI, xxxi.

l.97. *Sedgie Lee:* in order to defeat the Danes Alfred divided up the channel of the River Lea so as to deny it access to the sea. Hence the river moved slowly and its banks became sedgy (Spenser, *Prothalamion*, 118; *Polybn*, XVI, 299–310).

l.98. *Coaly Tine:* Newcastle was famous for its coal (*Polybn*, XXIX, 120–5). Milton's epithet here is bathetic and jocular, the poetical suffix -*y* giving mock dignity to the expression.

l.98. *ancient hallowed Dee:* the Dee was associated with the Druids of ancient Britain (cf. *FQ*, IV, XI, xxxix and *Polybn*, X, 200–8).

l.99. The six rivers of Yorkshire were supposed to have been six knights who were cruelly slain and drowned by a Scythian King Humber whence the river took its name (cf. *FQ*, IV, XI, xxxvii; and *Polybn*, XXVIII, 465–6).

l.100. *Medway smooth:* referring to the naval roads in the Medway which both Spenser (*FQ*, IV, XI, xlv; and Drayton (*Polybn*, XVIII, 86) call 'silver'.

l.100. *Royal Towred Thame:* Spenser (*FQ*, IV, XI, xxvii) refers to towers on the Thames though he is talking about Oxford. Milton is clearly referring to Windsor Castle to which Drayton refers in his account of the Thames (*Polybn*, XV, 313–20) though the latter says nothing about towers. The detail, though obvious enough, may be provided by Milton from his own knowledge of the Thames valley. The castle was built by Edward III.

26. THE PASSION

Written as the first stanza indicates soon after the *Nativity Ode* i.e. 1630. It is difficult to know why Milton included this fragment in the 1645 volume. Possibly because, with the *Nativity Ode* and *Upon the Circumcision*, it gives explicit evidence of his Christian piety even if it does not do it very well. Or he may have thought that it was not a bad example of a poetical exercise in a rather rhetorical manner even if it were not a very good example of a poem of Christian devotion. And characteristically the comment at the end—'finding [it] to be above the yeers he had'—draws attention to the precocity of his talents even if, this time, the attempt did not quite come off. The poem is in the manner of *On the Death of a Fair Infant* with its poetical language and its conceitedness, but this time the manner suits the subject even less. The striking of poetic attitudes is here particularly unseemly: the more Milton talks about the immensity of his subject and the more he emphasizes his own role as deeply moved spectator, the less capable does he become of doing justice either to the subject or to his feelings about it.

l.4. divide: a pun. Milton 'shared' his song with the angels in the *Nativity Ode,* but *divide* is also a musical term = 'descant'.

l.12. freely: without reluctance.

ll.13–14. Milton is implying that Christ's labours were more heroic and onerous than the twelve labours of Hercules which represented, in classical mythology, the utmost in difficulty and danger.

l.16. dropt: i.e. dripped. Milton is thinking of the anointing oil which was poured over the heads of the kings and priests of Israel in order to purify them (e.g. 2 Kings 9: 1–3).

l.18. front: forehead.

l.23. Phoebus: Greek Apollo, the god of poetry; but Milton also remembers his role as sun-god and hence calls the goal of the poem *this Horizon.*

l.26. Cremona's trump: a poetic periphrasis for the *Christiad,* an heroic poem on the life of Christ by Vida (1490–1566) who was born at Cremona.

l.28. still: soft in sound.

l.30. Pole: sky.

ll.34–5. Mourning poems were sometimes printed in white on black paper.

l.35. wannish: a pale, dull white i.e. (as is appropriate) not sparkling.

ll.36–7. The prophet Ezekiel by the river *Chebar* saw the chariot of God and was borne up in it (Ezekiel 1–3).

l.42. fit: a pun (i) part of a song; (ii) trance-like state.

l.43. i.e. the tomb where Christ was buried.

l.46. Quarry: large mass of stone.

l.47. lively: intensely, strikingly.

ll.48–9. A not very well managed conceit. One can see why Milton's tears might have to engrave his lament on the stone of the tomb if his hands are made powerless by grief, but he does not adequately explain why his tears should do any better or how they are instructed.

l.49. Characters: letters.

ll.50–6. Another rather over-ingenious conceit. That Milton might hear his grief echoed by the woods and waters is proper enough, but it is less satisfactory to imagine him beguiled by this into supposing that the clouds have given birth to mourners. If the death of Christ is all that distressing, it is easier to imagine that the clouds did indeed weep rather than to be beguiled into thinking that they did.

l.50. viewles: invisible.

l.51. cf. Jeremiah 9: 10.

28. ON TIME

Written circ. 1633.

In the *Trinity MS* the poem has the title 'To be set on a clock case'. It would thus seem to belong to that class of poems which is occasioned by the contemplation of familiar and domestic objects. Cf. for example Lord Herbert of Cherbury's poem 'To his watch when he could not sleep' which also concerns itself with thoughts of death and time. Milton's manner is however rather sublime for this sort of poem which may explain why the title 'On Time' was given to the poem instead. The metre may owe something to Italian poetry though stanzas of odes are often similar to this poem in the mixing of long and short lines and in close-linked though not regular-recurring rhyme. As a technical achievement this poem is superb, its skill being shown particularly in its structure and the way in which it leads to the ecstatic close.

l.3.   *heavy Plummets pace:* i.e. the movement of the clock's weight.

ll.4–6.   Time feeds merely on those things to which it itself gives birth i.e. seconds, minutes and those trivial things that belong to the transient as distinct from those that belong to the lasting world of the spirit. Milton's expression here is rather harshly conceited.

l.10.   A better because less clouded conceit. Time will eventually bring about its own final moment.

l.12.   *individual:* inseparable, not to be divided; hence everlasting.

l.14.   cf. *l*.9.

l.20.   *quit:* requited, paid for.

28. UPON THE CIRCUMCISION

Written circ. 1633. With the *Nativity Ode* and *The Passion* this poem makes up a group of poems on important events in Christ's life. Milton's intention at one time might have been to write a set of poems on these events as Donne did in his sonnet sequence *La Corona*. The feast of the circumcision (marking the circumcision of the Christ child (Luke 2: 21)) is on January 1st. The ceremony symbolized to the Jews acceptance of the blessings and obligations of the covenant which God had set up between Himself and Abraham and his descendants (Genesis 17). For the metre of this poem, cf. comments on *On Time* above.

ll.1–4.   As with *The Passion* the poem opens with a reference to the *Nativity Ode*.

ll.6–9.   A conceit on the idea of angelic mourning. Angelic essence is the

117

elements of fire and air which rise as distinct from those of water and earth which sink. Thus angels cannot weep tears made of water (cf. Milton's reference to the same idea in *Paradise Lost*, I, 620: 'Tears such as angels weep'). But they can sigh since they are made of air, though their sighs will be sighs of fire and unaccompanied by tears unless they borrow water from tears which have been wept on earth.

*l.*10. *all Heav'ns heraldry:* Christ's birth was announced with pomp and glory by the angels (Luke 2: 9–14).

*l.*10. *whilear:* a while ago. A poetical word.

*l.*11. *now bleeds:* bleeding is a necessary part of circumcision. St Paul (Romans 2: 25) had emphasized circumcision as a purification rite, but Milton makes a different and individual application of it seeing Christ's bleeding as a fore-runner of his eventual shedding of his blood for Man on the cross.

*l.*13. *sore:* a pun (i) because Christ suffers grievously at Man's sinfulness; (ii) because physical soreness was the result of circumcision (see for example, Genesis 34: 25).

*l.*15. *law more just:* i.e. the justice of God's doom of death on Man for his sinfulness.

*l.*20. *ev'n to nakednes:* cf. *Ecclesiastes*, 5: 15: 'As he came forth of his mother's womb, naked shall he return to go as he came.' *Nakednes* may also contain here the idea of Christ's poverty in His earthly state. To say that Christ '*emptied* His glory, ev'n to nakednes' is to juxtapose the ideas of emptiness and nakedness rather violently.

*l.*24. *excess:* grossly sinful behaviour i.e. Man's first disobedience.

30. AT A SOLEMN MUSICK

Written circ. 1633. In structure and manner very similar to *On Time* (see introductory note to that poem). It should be noted that this poem is not endorsing the idea of the music of the spheres at all (see *Nativity Ode*, 48) though it looks at times as though it is. Milton is writing a serious and explicit Christian poem describing the angelic song of joy in Heaven and looking to the time when Man, as he once did, will again take part in that song (*ll.*17–24). The writing, with its musical imagery appropriate to the occasion of a *Solemn Musick*, merely comes metaphorically close to the concept of the music of the spheres.

Title: A Solemn Musick: a musical performance of a festive or ceremonial nature

*l.*1. *Blest pair of Sirens:* The Sirens were originally sea-nymphs who by their melodious song charmed passing sailors to destruction. In Homer, *Odyssey*, XII, 39–184, Odysseus sails safely by them only by stopping up the ears of his comrades with wax and binding himself to the mast. There are two sirens in Homer but later writers generally made them three. A most important application of the myth is to be found in Plato, *Republic*, X. Plato writes of eight sirens, each sitting on a sphere of the heavens whose singing makes up the music of the spheres. This beneficent role for them is taken over by Milton though he reduces their number to Homer's two (with a mythological application of his own to *Voice and Vers*). His word *blest* indicates that these sirens are not those of a malignant kind.

l.1. *pledges:* i.e. tokens here on earth of the bliss that Man will eventually enjoy in Heaven.

l.2. *Sphear-born:* i.e. heavenly. Milton uses this word because he knows all about Plato's sirens.

l.4. i.e. able to move dead things by breathing sense into them.

l.5. *phantasie:* imagination. A pun is possibly intended since fantasy (fantasia) is also a piece of music.

l.6. *concent:* harmony.

l.7. *saphire-colour'd throne:* see Ezekiel 1: 26.

l.17. *undiscording:* undiscordant.

l.23. *Diapason:* harmony. A more technical musical term than concent (*l.6*).

l.27. *consort:* a harmonious combination of instruments and voices. Perhaps also a reference to the occasion of the poem.

31. AN EPITAPH ON THE MARCHIONESS OF WINCHESTER

Lady Jane Paulet (born 1607), Marchioness of Winchester, died in 1631 of an infection while she was pregnant of her second son. The family were Catholic though the Marchioness was, according to one report, 'inclining to become Protestant'. This poem is not an epitaph in the sense of a short poem which could be inscribed upon a tomb. An epitaph was more generally a poem lamenting and praising the dead and consoling the mourners. This poem is like *On Shakespear* and *Lycidas* in that Milton is one of many poets who wrote a poetical tribute. The manner of this poem— its neat octosyllabics, its elegance, its wit—shows the influence of Ben Jonson who himself wrote an elegy on the Marchioness.

l.3. her maternal grandfather was made Earl Rivers in 1626. The Earl had no surviving male children and so obtained the reversion of the peerage for his son-in-law Viscount Savage, the Marchioness's father.

l.18. *The God etc:* i.e. Hymen, the Greek god of marriage. He was usually represented as crowned with marjoram and roses and carrying a burning torch. Ovid, *Metamorphoses*, X, 4–7 represents Hymen as appearing at the wedding of Orpheus and Eurydice with a sputtering and smoky torch. This way of indicating a union that was to end tragically prompts Milton's invention here of a cypress (funereal) bud in Hymen's garland and a poorly burning torch.

l.26. *Lucina:* goddess who presided over the birth of children and particularly gave ease to the mother's labour.

l.26. *throws:* i.e. throes.

l.28. *Atropos:* one of three sisters, the Fates, who presided over the lives of men. Her name means 'stern' or 'implacable', and her particular duty was to bring about death by cutting the thread of life (cf. *Lycidas, ll*.75–6).

l.30. *fruit and tree:* i.e. child and mother.

l.35. *slip:* cutting of a plant. Milton's point is that he has seen a careless gardener, in mistake for some flower that has been brought out by a spring shower, pick and hence kill a plant which had been carefully nurtured throughout the winter.

l.49. *travel:* i.e. travail.

ll.55–60. Milton was still at Cambridge when this poem was written. He is referring obliquely to his poem as his tribute to her. It has been suggested that there was some idea of putting together an anthology of Cambridge pieces in honour of the Marchioness as was to be done later for Edward King (see *Lycidas*).

l.56. *Helicon:* mountain in Boeotia, Greece, sacred to the Muses.

l.57. *Bays:* laurel wreath, emblematic of success in war or poetry.

l.63. i.e. Rachel, daughter of Laban, for whom Jacob served fourteen years (Genesis 29). Ruth was barren for many years before she gave birth to Joseph (Genesis 30), and she died giving birth to her second child, Benjamin (Genesis 35). The Marchioness had married in 1622 and her first son was not born until 1630.

l.74. Milton wittily (though nonetheless movingly) shows how the dead marchioness's promotion in the spiritual state to a crown of life (Revelation 2: 10) is also a 'social' promotion from marchioness to queen.

34. SONG ON MAY MORNING

A song is a piece written to be set to music. As can be seen from this poem, simplicity is not a necessary characteristic: Milton's manner is formal, consciously poetical and literary.

34. ON SHAKESPEAR

This poem is one of the poems in honour of Shakespeare included in the Second Folio (1632). Milton was not named as the author. It was reprinted in *Poems: Written by Wil.Shake-speare. Gent.* in 1640, this time over the initials *I.M.* Milton invents a nice variant on the stock monument/death theme: it is not Shakespeare's works but his readers who are ingeniously shown to be the poet's best monuments. The point is made with some rather violent changes of metaphor.

l.4. y-pointing: an archaic formation of Milton's own, and improper since the prefix y- belongs to the past not the present (as here) participle. Shakespeare himself uses this sort of style to mark a deliberately old-fashioned (see *Pericles*, III, Prologue) or over-poetical (see *Love's Labours Lost*, I, i, 233ff.) manner.

l.8. livelong: long-lasting. A meaning peculiar to Milton and oddly applied here to make the point that Shakespeare's works last beyond the measure of his life. It is interesting that the 1632 text reads *lasting*.

ll.9–10. That Shakespeare was a poet of nature was a commonplace about him (cf. *L'Allegro*, 133–4).

l.10. and that: i.e. while.

l.11. leaves: a pun (i) pages; (ii) Delphi in Greece was the site of Apollo's most famous temple and oracle, and Milton is referring to the fact that the Cumaean Sybil, priestess of Apollo, on occasion wrote her prophecies on leaves.

l.11. unvalu'd: invaluable.

l.13. bereaving: depriving. The word does not at this time have the specific sense of 'depriving by the loss in death' which it has now.

l.14. too much conceaving: a paradox. The too extensive imagining (conceiving) is not a striking into life (conceiving) but a dying into marble.

35. ON THE UNIVERSITY CARRIER

Thomas Hobson was the university carrier (of goods and letters) who died in the Michaelmas vacation 1631 aged 86 years. His death was the occasion of a number of academic poems of a jocular kind, and Milton's own manner is broadly humourous and witty. Hobson was clearly a university 'character', so the fact that these two poems on him have nothing of the solemnity which Milton's other elegies on more distinguished people have implies no disrespect or contempt on Milton's part.

l.1. girt: saddle-girth.

l.4. slough: a very muddy place in the road.

l.5. shifter: a pun (i) carrier; (ii) 'shrewd customer'.

l.8. the Bull: Hobson's London terminal.

l.10. course of carriage: conveyance. It *fail'd* because it was the vacation.

l.13. latest: last.

l.14. Chamberlin: attendant at an inn.

36. ANOTHER ON THE SAME

ll.1–2. A logical (syllogistic) joke: life exists in motion; Hobson had kept himself alive (earned money) by carrying.

*l.*4. *keep his trot:* perhaps a pun. *Trot* was jocular for an old woman. None of the other Hobson poems refer to a wife, but Milton's point might be that Hobson keeps only a horse's trot.

*l.*5. *sphear-metal:* i.e. substance of which the heavenly spheres were made, and hence indestructible. The joke is that there was much dispute about the composition of the spheres.

*ll.*7–8. That time measures motion was an old philosophical idea. Motion measured Hobson's time because he spent his days carrying.

*ll.*9–10. Hobson had no work in the vacation.

*l.*12. *breathing:* rest (cf. mod. 'breather').

*l.*17. *swooning bed:* The bed also swooned because Hobson was such a big man (see *l.*20).

*l.*18. *fetch't:* a pun (i) carried; (ii) restored to consciousness.

*l.*19. *cross:* opposed to his refusal to get well.

*ll.*29–31. Hobson plied regularly, going to and fro like the tide, and no doubt also handled goods that came from abroad.

*l.*32. A paradox depending upon the pun in *wain:* (i) cart; (ii) the waning of the moon reduces its size.

*l.*34. *superscription:* a pun (i) an inscription; hence an epitaph (like this poem); (ii) address on a letter, reading which had been a necessary part of Hobson's business.

L'ALLEGRO and IL PENSEROSO

This poem and its companion *Il Penseroso* are poems of pure delight. They offer a series of pleasing pictures to the mind—*L'Allegro* celebrating the delights that come from mirth and shared pleasures by day and night, *Il Penseroso* celebrating those that come from contemplation and solitude through those same times. Their different attitudes are sometimes shown towards the same things e.g. plays; at other times the pleasure is peculiar to one of them, e.g. the farmyard scene in *L'Allegro* or the college cloister in *Il Penseroso*. The two poems are to be judged by the fitness of the way in which they represent and communicate their different moods and tastes, by their combination of discipline and ease, by their freedom from vulgarity and coarseness, by their witty elegance and clarity. They keep a nice balance between the natural and the poetical. One of their achievements is that they seem so effortlessly original. Although they make no apparent display of originality it is impossible to find poems that are quite like them. As Johnson said of Pope's *Rape of the Lock*: 'New things are made familiar, and familiar things are made new.' They were written some time in the first half of the 1630's. It is impossible to date them precisely.

Title: L'Allegro means 'the lively, gay man'. It is difficult to see why Milton gave these two poems Italian titles. Perhaps with this one he wished to match *Il Penseroso*, a description that would have more currency. And perhaps he thought that the Italian would add to the poems' air of culture and elegance.

ll.1–10. Milton opens with a rejection of melancholy. The picture he here draws of melancholy is a deliberately black one, carried through in a light, rather highly poetical manner.

l.2. Cerberus: the dog which according to Greek mythology guarded the gateway to the underworld.

l.3. Stygian: the Styx was the river of the underworld.

l.5. uncouth: unknown i.e. lonely.

l.8. Ebon: ebony-coloured i.e. black. A poetical expression.

l.8. *low brow'd*: i.e. overhanging. The compound is of Milton's own making. The arch (brow) of the rocks is very low and thus dark.

l.9. *ragged*: rough.

l.10. *Cimmerian*: the Cimmerii were a people who the Greeks supposed lived in perpetual darkness in the farthest west of the ocean (see *Odyssey*, XI, 12–19).

l.11. *free*: of noble birth.

l.12. *ycleap'd*: called. A very common poetical archaism.

l.12. *Euphrosyne*: one of the Graces, three beautiful maidens, daughters of Bacchus and Venus, who attended upon Venus. The word *Euphosyne* means 'mirth'.

l.16. *Ivy-crowned*: the ivy was sacred to Bacchus since he was the god of wine.

ll.17–24. *Zephir*, the west wind, and husband of Flora, goddess of flowers, is usually Aurora's son, but Greek mythology gives varying accounts of the parentage etc. of minor gods, and Milton here clearly feels free to invent his own genealogy for his goddess Mirth. Thus his phrase *as som Sager sing* is a bit of fun since the matter seems to be wholly of his own invention.

l.24. *bucksom*: full of delight.

l.24. *debonair*: pleasant in appearance and manner.

l.27. *Quips and Cranks*: verbal jests and tricks.

l.29. *Hebe*: goddess of youth who was Jove's cupbearer (cf. *At a Vacation Exercise*, *l*.38).

l.34. *fantastick*: the word meant 'imaginary, quaint in conception'. Milton here gives it a quite especial new sense: 'lively (in movement)'.

l.36. *Mountain Nymph, sweet Liberty*: the Oreads were mountain nymphs. To identify one of them as Liberty is original to Milton, but logical enough.

l.43. *dappled*: streaked with various colours. A poetical word.

l.44. *in spite of*: in defiance of.

l.55. *Hoar*: grey, perhaps because the shadows have not fully gone. A poetical usage.

l.59. i.e. directly facing the portals of the Dawn; with the dawn sky in full view.

l.61. *Amber*: yellow. A poetical word.

l.62. *dight*: dressed. A common poetical archaism.

l.67. *tells his tale*: an activity as much reminiscent of the activities of shepherds in pastoral poetry as of the shepherds of actual life. The meaning is also possibly 'counts his sheep'.

l.70. *Lantskip*: common 16–18th century spelling of 'landscape'.

l.71. i.e. reddish-brown fields and grey ploughed land. A difficult, though not impossible, scene to envisage. *Russet* could also be used to signify a grey colour. *Russet Lawns* is poetical.

*l.*74. *labouring:* moving heavily. Milton achieves some wit here: *Labouring* also means 'suffering the pains of childbirth' which gives a nice contrast with *barren brest.*

*l.*78. *Boosom'd:* enclosed. A very picturesque usage.

*l.*78. *tufted:* clustered. A use original to Milton.

*l.*80. *Cynosure:* a very poetical expression. *Cynosure* is the constellation of the Great Bear and here is used figuratively to signify something that attracts by its beauty.

*l.*83. *Corydon:* a shepherd in Theocritus and Virgil.

*l.*83. *Thyrsis:* a shepherdess in Virgil.

*l.*85. *Messes:* a simple meal such as a peasant might eat.

*l.*86. *Phillis:* countrywoman in Virgil's *Eclogues.*

*l.*88. *Thestylis:* countrywoman in Virgil's *Eclogues.*

*l.*90. *tann'd:* sunburnt.

*l.*91. *secure:* carefree.

*l.*94. *rebecks:* fiddles.

*l.*99. *live-long:* very long since it is midsummer (see *On Shakespear, l.*8).

*l.*102. *Faery Mab:* Queen Mab of the fairies (see *Romeo and Juliet,* I, iv, *ll.* 53–94).

*l.*102. *junkets:* sweetmeats, cakes.

*l.*103. *She:* i.e. one of the women present at the gathering where these stories are told (*ll.*100–1).

*l.*104. *Friars Lanthorn:* i.e. the ignis fatuus or phosphorescent marsh-gas popularly supposed to lead travellers astray.

*l.*105. *drudging Goblin:* Puck/Robin Goodfellow. For an account of his tricks see Shakespeare, *Midsummer Night's Dream,* II, i, 32–57. Milton's goblin is more of a giant than Shakespeare's and his gift is in strength not swiftness. Nor does Shakespeare include this particular task (*ll.*105–9) among Puck's feats, but the fairy achievement in one night of a task that would take men many days to do is common in fairy stories.

*l.*110. *Lubbar:* drudging.

*l.*113. *Crop-full:* i.e. having eaten his fill of the *Cream-bowl* (*l.*106) that is the reward for his night's labours. *Crop* is a very vigorous word, and the compound is of Milton's making.

*l.*122. *influence:* see *Nativity Ode, l.*71 note. The primary meaning of influence gives Milton's verb *rain* some forcefulness and point.

*l.*125. *Hymen:* c.f. *Epitaph on the Marchioness of Winchester. ll.*18–22, note. *Hymen* is presented as wearing a saffron robe in Ovid, *Metamorphoses,* X, 1.

*l.*128. *mask:* a courtly entertainment. See introductory note to *Comus.*

*l.*132. *Jonson's learned Sock:* actors in comedy on the classical stage wore light shoes as distinct from the heavy shoe (buskin) of tragedy. Jonson's comedies were written in accordance with classical precedent and so are much more obviously triumphs of learning than the more 'natural' comedies of Shake-speare (cf. *On Shakespear*, 9–10).

l.133. fancy's childe: the *fancy* is the poetical imagination, a quality of nature, which Milton is here distinguishing from those poetic qualities which come from instruction and learning.

l.134. Warble: sing. A poetical word.

l.135. against: as a protection against.

l.136. Lydian: one of the modes of Greek music characterized by its softness and sweetness.

l.138. meeting: responsive.

l.138. pierce: pronounced 'perse'. A violent word when juxtaposed with *meeting* and *winding bout*.

l.139. bout: an action (here a piece of music) such as may be heard at one time without interruption. The earlier sense of 'roundabout way' no doubt helped to give Milton his epithet *winding*.

l.141. wanton heed and giddy cunning: paradoxes appropriate to the 'natural' effect which 'art' often conveys.

l.143. Untwisting all the chains: Untwisting is aptly used of the effect of music: 'Breaking the chains' would be too violent and inappropriate.

l.145. Orpheus: mythological Greek poet, the son of the Muse Calliope, who was given his lyre by Apollo himself. His song had the power to charm rocks and beasts so to say that Orpheus himself would be roused from slumber is a witty and poetic way of indicating the quality of the music that Milton is here describing. Orpheus went to the underworld to attempt to bring back his wife *Eurydice*. His song so charmed *Pluto*, the king of the underworld, that he agreed to let Eurydice go provided that Orpheus did not look back at her until he was past the gates of the underworld. Orpheus forgot his promise and looked back and so lost his wife. Eurydice was thus *half-regained* by the charm of Orpheus's music, and Milton develops a nice invention by supposing that the music he is describing would have gone one better and persuaded Pluto *to have quite set free* Eurydice.

41. IL PENSEROSO

See introductory note to *L'Allegro*.

Title: i.e. 'the contemplative, thoughtful man'. Michelangelo's statue of Lorenzo de Medici had been known under this name.

ll.1–10. the cheerful man of *L'Allegro* would find this a misrepresentation of what he meant by joy. Cf. *L'Allegro*, *ll.1–10* note.

l.2. without father: i.e. of monstrous birth.

l.3. bested: help.

l.10.   *Pensioners:* attendants at court, retainers. There is some wit in the phrase *fickle Pensioners:* (i) courts are haunts of inconstancy and insincerity; (ii) one would expect the risk of fickleness to come rather from the person giving the pension than the person receiving it.

l.10.   *Morpheus:* god of sleep.

l.14.   *hit the sense:* a vigorous expression. Cf. *Samson Agonistes*, 1568.

ll.13–16.   An ingenious conceit to rid Melancholy of the wrong implications of her association with black.

l.18.   *Prince Memnon's sister:* Hemera. Memnon was a king of Ethiopia (and hence *black*) who chivalrously brought an army to assist the Trojans towards the end of the Trojan War.

l.19.   *that starr'd Ethiope Queen:* i.e. Cassiope (or Cassiopea), queen of Cepheus, king of Ethiopia. She boasted that she was fairer than the sea-nymphs, and was punished by Neptune's sending a beast to ravage her country at the nymphs' request. At her death she was made a constellation in the southern hemisphere.

ll.22–30.   As in *L'Allegro ll*.14–24 Milton invents an apt and poetic genealogy for his goddess.

l.23.   *Vesta:* Roman goddess of the hearth and home whose temple was served by virgin priestesses. She was the same as the Greek Hestia who was a daughter of Cronos (Roman Saturn) and Rhea. In the light of her association with virginity there is some wit in Milton's invention that she had a daughter by her own father. *Saturn* ruled in Olympus before he was deposed by *Jove* his son. He fled to Italy and ruled there for a time. This period (*Saturns raign*) which came to be known as the Golden Age (see *Nativity Ode, l*.135) was distinguished for its virtue and happiness. But Saturn also suffered at the hands of Jove (hence *fear of Jove*) by whom he was for some time imprisoned beneath the earth and sea. Saturn is usually represented as old and infirm, and he was associated with melancholy and time. Milton here emphasizes Saturn as the ruler in the Golden Age and describes him as *solitary* in order to point up a useful association with his own contemplative man.

l.27.   *glimmering:* shining faintly. A poetical word.

l.29.   *Ida:* a beautiful and famous mountain near Troy, supposed to be frequented by the gods.

l.32.   *demure:* grave, serious. The sense of a rather provocative seriousness of manner did not develop until the later 17th century.

l.31.   *Nun:* priestess, not necessarily of a Christian order.

l.33.   *grain:* colour. A poetical word.

l.35.   *Cipres Lawn:* dark (like the cypress tree) fine linen.

l.36.   *decent:* comely.

ll.41–4.   Milton's conceit is that Melancholy by her commerce with the heavens will acquire a steadfast contempt for the things of earth. As in *ll*.13–16 he is presenting an ingenious explanation of a stock image of his goddess, in this case of a dull and inert (*Leaden*) person whose eyes are forever fixed on the ground. He argues that Melancholy is really like a monument, made of marble but fixed (as is necessary) to the ground with lead. So *cast* is a pun: (i) look, expression; (ii) mould (into which metal is poured).

l.47.   *Muses:* see *Nativity Ode, l.15* note. The Muses were traditionally presented as dancing round Jove's altar.

l.50.   *trim:* properly made and kept.

ll.52–4.   Milton is adapting the vision in Ezekiel 10 of the chariot of God. He reduces the four cherubim by the wheels to one who is the driver and who is (rather unscripturally) identified as *Contemplation.*

l.55.   *hist:* summon in silence. The verb is formed (apparently by Milton himself) from the interjection 'hist'.

l.56.   *Philomel:* i.e. the nightingale. Philomela was the sister of Procne who married Tereus, king of Thrace. Tereus fell in love with Philomela, but she rejected his advances. The two sisters revenged themselves on Tereus by murdering his son. Tereus was about to kill them for this act when all three were changed into birds, Tereus into a hoopoe, Procne into a swallow and Philomela into a nightingale. In the melancholy of the nightingale's and the swallow's song one is supposed to hear the two sisters lamenting the unhappiness they suffered in life. (For the story, see Ovid, *Metamorphoses,* VI, 421–674.) Later, the nightingale was associated with unhappiness and loneliness in love (cf. Milton's *Sonnet* I).

l.58.   *rugged:* rough-haired.

l.59.   *Cynthia:* see *Nativity Ode, l.103.* In classical mythology she is usually presented as having winged horses yoked to her chariot (Ceres, the goddess of harvest, had dragons) but the traditional associations of dragons and night led to Renaissance presentations of her with dragons (cf. Marlowe, *Hero and Leander,* I, 107; Shakespeare, *Midsummer Night's Dream,* III, ii, 379).

l.60.   *accustom'd:* perhaps because Milton wishes to stress the regular and habitual nature of the contemplative man.

l.66.   *smooth-shaven:* this use of *shaven* in connection with grass and not hair is poetical.

l.68.   *noon:* i.e. the moon's position in the sky at midnight.

l.67.   *wandring:* i.e. moving with apparently no fixed course. The planets in Greek and Latin are called the 'wandering stars'.

l.73.   *Plat:* patch.

l.74.   *Curfeu:* warning bell rung at a fixed hour in the evening, originally as a signal to douse all domestic fires. The sea here is part of the poetical setting that Milton aptly provides and has no other connection with the bell.

l.76.   *sullen:* mournful. A poetical usage. *Roar* is a rather strange word to use of the mournful sound of a bell. The necessity of rhyme may have been responsible for it.

*l.*80.   A paradox. The smouldering ashes of the fire barely serve to lighten the darkness. *Gloom* is poetical (cf. *Nativity Ode*, *l.*77 note).

*l.*83.   *Belmans drowsie charm:* the nightwatchmen would recite formulae calling for blessing and protection on the houses and their dwellers as they passed along the streets at night. See, for example, Herrick's two poems 'The Bellman'.

*l.*87.   *outwatch the Bear:* i.e. stay awake all night. The Great Bear constellation remains in the sky all night.

*l.*88.   *thrice great Hermes:* i.e. Hermes Trismagistus (=Hermes Thrice-greatest). Hermes in Greek mythology was the god of arts and sciences, and Hermes Trismagistus was the name given to the Egyptian god Thoth who was identified with the Greek god Hermes. It was believed in the Renaissance that there were two divinely inspired sources of wisdom: (i) the Bible and (ii) a body of writings supposed to have been handed down from ancient times by Hermes Trismagistus, thence down to Plato etc. Thus Milton presents himself as reading these writings here because through them he can attain a knowledge of the divine mysteries of the universe.

*l.*88.   *unsphear/The spirit of Plato:* take the soul of Plato from the sphere to which it had gone after death. In the *Phaedo* Plato argues that the souls of the virtuous rise to the upper regions of fire and air after death (cf. *Comus*, *ll.*1-5).

*ll.*88-92.   Milton's use of Platonic material in this passage suits the poetical elegance of *Il Penseroso*. Explicit Christian doctrine would strike too harsh and severe a note for his purpose.

*l.*93.   *Dæmons:* in Greek mythology supernatural beings whose nature was midway between that of gods and men.

*l.*94.   i.e. in all of the four elements (air, fire, water and earth) of which, according to ancient and medieval science, the world was composed.

*l.*95.   *consent:* harmony.

*l.*96.   i.e. they are creatures of both sky and earth.

*l.*98.   *Scepter'd Pall:* the sceptre and the pall are emblematic of the dignity and richness of tragedy and emphasize the concern of classical tragedy with kings and heroes of high rank. Milton puts the two emblems together rather violently in this expression.

*l.*99.   *Thebs:* famous city of Greece, the tragic lives of whose early kings (e.g. Oedipus) formed the subject matter of many Greek dramas.

*l.*99.   *Pelops line:* Pelops in Greek legend was king of Pisa in Greece. His descendants were cursed by Myrtilius who, because he had insulted Pelops' wife, was cast into the sea by him. The horrors that beset the lives of his descendants as a result of the curse are the subjects of many Greek tragedies.

*l.*100.   i.e Homer's *Iliad* and *Odyssey* which, though epics, narrate the misfortunes arising out of the Trojan War.

*l.*101.   *(though rare):* Milton has a low opinion of post-classical drama.

*l.*101. *Ennobled:* in two senses (i) given dignity and fame to, (ii) been about heroes of high birth.

*l.*102. *Buskind stage:* i.e. tragic drama. See *L'Allegro*, *l.*132.

*l.*103. *sad Virgin:* i.e. Melpomene, the Muse of Tragedy.

*l.*104. *Musaeus:* Mythical founder of Greek poetry, the son or pupil of Orpheus. Virgil (*Aeneid*, VI, 667–8) presents him in the Elysian fields as the most illustrious of mortal poets.

*ll.*105–8. See *L'Allegro*, note.

*l.*107. *Iron tears:* a violent expression to convey Pluto's sternness.

*l.*109. *him that left untold:* i.e. Chaucer. The reference is to the *Squire's Tale* which Chaucer left unfinished. The story concerns King *Cambuscan* of Tartarye who had two sons, *Camball* and *Algarsife*, and a daughter *Canace*. During a court feast a knight entered bearing strange gifts from his lord, the King of Arabe and Inde. The gifts were a brass horse that had the power of incredibly speedy flight for Cambuscan; for Canace a magic mirror that could reveal the future and a ring which gave its wearer the power to talk to birds; and lastly a sword that could cut through anything. It is a romantic story concerned with magic, war and love. Spenser continued it in *The Faerie Queene*, IV. Milton's inclusion of this story here shows that his contemplative man is not over-solemn in his tastes.

*l.*113. *vertuous:* endowed with wondrous power.

*l.*117. *solemn:* inspiring grave thoughts.

*l.*120. *meets the ear:* i.e. is heard. A phrase apparently original to Milton.

*l.*119. *drear:* doleful. A poetical word.

*l.*122. *civil-suited:* sober and graceful in dress.

*l.*123. *trickt:* artfully dressed.

*l.*123. *frounc't:* with curled hair.

*l.*124. *Attic boy:* i.e. Cephalus, prince of Thessaly, who was fond of hunting. Aurora, the goddess of the dawn, fell in love with hm when she saw him out hunting one day. According to Ovid, *Metamorphoses*, VII, 700–13 he rejected her advances, but other accounts say that they had a son Phaeton. Attica is a part of Greece.

*l.*126. *Cherchef't:* with a garment covering her breasts and shoulders; hence she is *comely:* seemly, decorous, as befits the tone here.

*l.*132. *flaring:* shining brightly and fitfully.

*l.*134. *Sylvan:* Roman god of the woods.

*l.*135. *monumental:* i.e. large and impressive. A poetical expression.

*l.*141. *Day's garish eie:* i.e. the excessively bright sun.

*l.*142. *the Bee with Honied thie:* an idea found in Drayton and Shakespeare, *Midsummer Night's Dream* III, i, 172.

*l.*145. *such consort:* i.e. such great unison.

*l.*146. *dewy-featherd:* i.e. gentle-winged (because dew falls lightly).

*ll.*147–50.   Very difficult lines. (i) *Wave at his wings:* wings would seem more properly to wave rather than be waved at; (ii) *his:* whose? Sleep's or the dream's? probably in view of *l.*146 it is Sleep's; (iii) *of lively portrature:* probably = in/by means of life-like portrayal; (iv) *display'd:* does this qualify *Wings* or *portrature?* It can mean 'spread open to view' or 'expanded (like wings)'; (v) *laid:* does this qualify *Wings* or *portrature?* The general picture of sleep and dreams (cf. Ovid, *Metamorphoses*, XI, 592–649 on the Cave of Sleep and Morpheus) that Milton is aiming at is clear enough, but the sequence of ideas and syntax seems to have got confused.

*l.*148.   *Airy stream:* poetical for 'stream of air'.

*l.*154.   *Genius of the Wood:* i.e. spirit of the wood. Cf. *Nativity Ode*, *l.*186.

*ll.*155–66.   A highly poeticised version of college life.

*l.*156.   *Cloisters pale:* either (i) dim cloisters or (ii) the enclosure of the cloisters.

*l.*157.   *embowed:* arched.

*l.*158.   A difficult line. Possibly with the weighty (*massy*) experience of its strangely carved pillars.

*l.*159.   *storied:* representing sacred stories and legends.

*l.*159.   *dight:* adorned. A poetical archaism.

*l.*163.   *clear:* (i) audible and (ii) pure.

*l.*170.   *spell:* engage in study or contemplation. A poetical usage.

THE SONNETS

The sonnet was one of the most important literary forms in the Renaissance. Originating in Italy, it was established in England in the 16th century. Its two most common themes were love and religious devotion. The challenge of the form was in the craftsmanship that it required: a good sonnet had to be a triumph of logical arrangement. The popularity of the sonnet declined in the early part of the 17th century so that Milton is somewhat unusual in using the form as late as he did. On the other hand, his own close involvement with Italy and with Italian culture and poetry probably account for his rather unmodish interest in the form. His use of the sonnet to praise his heroic contemporaries is probably derived from Tasso. The form of the sonnet which Milton uses is the Petrarchan, i.e. the first 8 lines rhyme abbaabba while the sestet is varied. Milton does not divide the sonnet rigidly into octet and sestet, but handles the form with considerable freedom and variety. For the most part his sonnets have intensity and seriousness and lack the decorative, mythological character of much of the other poetry in this volume. This is probably because most of them were written much later than most of the other poems. Indeed sonnets are the only short poems that Milton wrote in the 1640's and 1650's. The form, combining art and brevity, was very useful to a man heavily involved with political employment and prose controversy and perhaps with the writing of his epic *Paradise Lost*.

Because of their connection with political events and persons of the Commonwealth *Sonnets XV, XVI, XVII*, and *XXII* were not included in the 1673 edition. They were first published together by Edward Phillips in his edition of Milton's *Letters of State* in 1694. (Only *Sonnet XVII* had been published before, in a life of Vane in 1662.) The text of these sonnets is taken from the *Trinity MS*, a manuscript, chiefly in Milton's own hand, which is in the Library of Trinity College, Cambridge, and which contains many of Milton's shorter poems. The inclusion of these sonnets means that the sonnets after *XIV* are numbered in accordance with the *Trinity MS* and not with 1673.

47. SONNET I

This is Milton's only conventional love poem. The plaintive note and the assertions about fidelity to Love and to the Muse are altogether conventional. It is usually dated circ. 1629.

l.1. *Nightingale:* see *Il Penseroso, l.*56 note.

l.2. *bloomy spray:* flowery small branch. A poetical phrase.

l.4. *hours:* see *Comus, l.*985 note.

l.6. Hearing the nightingale before the cuckoo was supposed to portend success in love; hearing the cuckoo first, the reverse.

l.6. *First heard:* i.e. if they are first heard.

l.6. *shallow:* foolish.

l.9. *the rude bird of Hate:* i.e. the cuckoo.

l.11. *as:* since.

SONNETS II–VI

These sonnets, not printed in this edition, are in Italian. They are love poems of devotion and compliment, addressed to an Italian girl named Emilia. It is impossible to say whether they represent real or merely poetical devotion. They are usually dated circ. 1629.

47. SONNET VII

This sonnet was included in a letter which Milton wrote to a friend in 1633. In the letter Milton is concerned about how little serviceable his life up to that time has been. The reason, he says, is that he is still undecided how best to serve God. Milton's problem of course has not to do with poetry. The sonnet is written with grave fluency and without ornament. Moral self-examination not elegance is the effect that Milton wishes to achieve.

l.2. The image is of a bird of prey which has snatched his twenty-third year so quickly (*soon*).

ll.5–8. I am perhaps older than I look, and in the same way the inner maturity I have may not be as obvious in my case as it is in the case of other people who are happy to find their deeds match their capacity.

l.8. this clause qualifies *inward ripeness.*

l.8. *timely-happy:* gratified at the proper time.

l.8. *indu'th:* endows, clothes visibly.

ll.13–14. In the eye of God all time is as eternity (*ever*). Because God does not live in time, He is hardly likely to be bothered as to whether Milton acts sooner or later (so long as he acts); God does not much mind about this twenty-third birthday.

48. SONNET VIII

The Royalist army was threatening London late in 1642. If, as the first deleted *Trinity MS* title seems to suggest, this sonnet was pinned up on Milton's door then, for all its putting on the style, it may be rather jocular. Certainly, it would be helpful to see the poem as intended jokingly as there is something unattractive about Milton's claiming exemption as a poet from the perils of a war whose cause he vehemently espoused.

ll.5–8. The ability of the poet to confer fame was a conventional theme.

ll.10–12. Alexander the Great of Macedon (for which *Emathia* was a poetical name) spared the house of the poet Pindar when he destroyed the city of Thebes.

ll.12–14. Plutarch ('Life of Lysander') relates that when a few lines of a tragic drama of Euripides (the writer of *Electra*) were recited (*repeated*) to the Spartan general Lysander during a council of war that was determining the fate of Athens, he was so moved that he decided not to desolate (*ruin bare*) the whole of a city that could foster such distinguished citizens, but simply to destroy its fortifications. Milton's use of *walls* here for 'houses' is somewhat inept since Lysander did destroy the fortifications of Athens.

48. SONNET IX

It is not known to whom this sonnet is addressed. It does not present us with an account of a specific person or of specific virtues. The solemnity of its style is emphasized by its Biblical allusions. It is usually dated circ. 1645.

l.2. *the broad way* leads to destruction (Matthew 7: 13), and the righteous inherit the desolate and high places of earth (Isaiah 49: 9).

l.3. *eminently:* a pun (i) notably; (ii) in high places (see note above).

l.5. *Mary . . . Ruth:* both types of lowly, virtuous steadfastness. (See Luke 1: 48; Ruth 2: 11–12.)

l.8. i.e. they love their enemies. See Matthew 5: 44.

ll.9–14. For the parable of the wise virgins who trimmed their lamps for the Lord's coming, see Matthew 25: 1–13.

l.10. *feastful friends:* friends who accompany him to the feast.

49. SONNET X

This is a much more specific sonnet than the previous one though its actual references are rather elusive without the deleted title in the *Trinity MS.* The Lady Margaret Ley was the daughter of James Ley, Earl of

Marlborough. She was married to John Hobson, a captain in the Parliamentary army, and she and her husband were friends of Milton's. Her father (1552–1629) was a lawyer and judge and was appointed Lord High Treasurer in 1624. He resigned this post in 1628 because he felt unable to support the King's request for money for the expedition to the Isle of Rhé (something that may have endeared him to Milton). He served as President of the Council for one year in 1628. The sonnet is one of graceful compliment to the father and daughter. Not all estimates of the Earl of Marlborough are as favourable as Milton's. The sonnet is usually dated circ. 1645.

l.4. He resigned both offices.

l.5. the sad breaking of that Parlament: Charles I dismissed Parliament in 1628 and ruled without it for thirteen years. That the Earl's death was connected with this event is Milton's own complimentary invention.

l.6. dishonest: shameful.

l.7. Chaeronea: Philip of Macedon's defeat of the Athenians at Chaeronea in Greece in the 4th century B.C. so overwhelmed the 99-year-old orator Isocrates (Milton's prose tract *Areopagitica* is based upon an oration of his) that he fasted and died.

49. SONNET XI

Milton's divorce tract *Tetrachordon* was published in 1645. The title (a word used in English only by Milton) means 'four-stringed' and refers to the four places in the Bible where the institution of marriage is discussed. The sonnet adopts a vehement style, reflected also in its violent enjambements and its wrenched rhymes. It is usually dated circ. 1646.

l.2. True of Milton's book. He is concerned with a very close analysis of the meaning and relationship of the Biblical texts.

l.4. Numbring good intellects: indicating by the number of its readers the number of intelligent readers.

ll.8–9. The alliance of Parliament with the Scots must have made Scottish names more familiar to English ears. They can hardly come more Scottish than some of these names of Milton's.

l.7. spelling false: misunderstanding.

l.10. the metaphor is of hair which is rough (*rugged*) made close and smooth (*sleek*).

l.11. Quintilian: Roman writer and rhetorician. English was regarded as a less musical language than Latin.

ll.12–14. Sir John Cheke (1514–1577) was a humanist and reformer. He was the first Regius Professor of Greek in Cambridge and was tutor to Edward VI.

Usually dated circ. 1646.

l.2. Milton characteristically insists on the rationality of his ideas about marriage and divorce. By the *rules of antient liberty* he means not precedent and authority but the principles of reason and nature upon which true liberty is based. In 1643 Parliament had passed an order under which all books had to be officially licensed and examined before printing. Milton's own divorce writings looked likely to get into trouble under this system, and his *Areopagitica* was written (1644) in defence of freedom of publication.

ll.5–7. *Latona* had the twins Apollo and Diana (later to become the sun and moon gods, *l.*6) by Jupiter. She was persecuted by Juno and forced to wander over the earth. At one point she asked the peasants in Caria (Asia Minor) for water, and, when they refused and reviled her, she asked Jupiter to punish them and they were changed into frogs (see Ovid, *Metamorphoses*, VI, 317–81).

l.7. *held . . . in fee:* exercised sovereignty over.

l.8. See Matthew 7: 6.

l.11. *Licence:* a pun (i) unbridled freedom (in *Areopagitica* Milton was careful to point out that his aim was liberty, not licence); (ii) licencing i.e. registration and control of printing.

l.12. Milton always held that political freedom was only properly held by those who were wise and virtuous. Cf. *Comus*, *ll.*763–6.

l.14. *for:* during: possibly 'in spite of'.

50. TO MR H. LAWES ON HIS AIRES
SONNET XIII

First published in an edition of some of Lawes's psalm music, 1648.

It is dated 1646 in the *Trinity MS*.

Another sonnet of graceful compliment. Henry Lawes (1596–1662) was the most successful and accomplished musician of the English court. He held offices in the Chapel Royal and was acquainted with many literary men. He set works of Herrick, Waller, Carew, and other poets of the time to music. The sonnet was first published as a complimentary poem in Lawes's *Choice Psalms put into Musick for Three Voices*, 1648. It is dated 1646 in the *Trinity MS*. See also introduction to *Arcades* and *Comus*.

l.1. *Harry:* familiar mode of address for Henry.

l.2. *span:* measure.

ll.3–4. Midas's judgement that Pan was a better musician than Apollo led to the latter's changing him into an ass.

l.4.   committing: associating long and short syllables incongruously together. There is possibly also a (hint of the) sense of 'committing a crime'.

l.10.   *Phoebus:* i.e. Apollo, god of music.

l.11.   *Story:* Lawes did set a narrative poem, *Ariadne deserted by Theseus,* to music.

ll.12–14.   When he arrived in Purgatory (Canto II) Dante saw his friend the musician Casella being conducted there. Dante asked Casella to sing to him so as to soothe his soul which had been distressed by its journey through Hell. Appropriately, Casella sings one of Dante's own songs which he had set to music.

51. SONNET XIV

An elegiac sonnet of rather vague praise. According to the deleted title in the *Trinity MS* it was written in memory of Mrs Catherine Thomason, who was the wife of George Thomason, a Presbyterian bookseller who was a friend of Milton's. The language and references are appropriately Biblical. It is usually dated circ. 1646.

l.4.   see, for example, John 5: 24.

ll.9–14.   The imagery is based on Exodus 25 and Revelation 8 and 22.

52. ON THE LORD GEN. FAIRFAX ETC.
SONNET XV

The next three sonnets were not included in the 1673 volume because of their obvious connection with political events of the Civil War and Commonwealth. See introductory note to Sonnets.

Thomas Fairfax (1612–67) was one of the most important figures on the Parliamentary side in the Civil War. In 1645 he was appointed Commander-in-Chief of the army and in this capacity he organized the New Model Army which brought the First Civil War to a close with its defeat of the King at Naseby in 1645. When the Second Civil War broke out the Scots invaded England in support of the King but were defeated at Preston. Fairfax was given the task of saving London from the Royalist insurrection in Kent. He defeated the Royalist army and then besieged Colchester where the Royalist leaders had taken refuge. Fairfax was a moderate politically and opposed to the execution of the King in 1649. He lived in retirement after this but played a major part in helping Monk's invasion of England from Scotland in 1659 which brought about the restoration of Charles II. Milton praised the heroic qualities of Fairfax in his *Second Defence of the English People* (1654) where he celebrated the heroes of the Revolution.

l.7. Hydra heads: the Hydra was a hundred-headed monster that was
eventually destroyed by Hercules.

ll.7–8. The Scottish support of the King was a breach of the terms of the
alliance which they had made with the Parliament.

ll.7–8. displaies: possibly a pun since it can mean 'spread (wings)'.

ll.7–8. impe their serpent wings: improve feathers of a bird so as to strengthen
its flight. Milton's contempt for the Scots' treachery is shown in that they do
this with a *broken league* and in his epithet *serpent* (i.e. dragon) which continues
the monstrosity of *Hydra*. The Hydra is not usually a serpent but Euripides
(*Ion*, v, 198) makes it so.

52. TO THE LORD GENERALL CROMWELL ETC.
SONNET XVI

Cromwell (1599–1658) slowly emerged as the most powerful of the
Parliamentary leaders during the Civil War. He was a brilliant general and
administrator. He was the leader of the Independents (i.e. those who
believed that each local congregation was an independent church) and his
power lay in his leadership of the Army which was largely Independent in
outlook. Once the Army had started to interfere in political matters it
found it difficult to stop, and the political history of the Commonwealth
lies in the various attempts which Cromwell made to set up a Parliament
which could work harmoniously with himself and the Army. Though his
rule became increasingly unpopular Milton never wavered in his support
for him. He regarded him (as this sonnet shows) as the man most likely to
solve the political and religious problems of England.

In 1652, in pursuit of a religious settlement, John Owen and other
ministers had made proposals for reform, and a committee of the Parliament
was appointed to consider them. The central issue was that of establishment
(i.e. regulation of the church and payment of the clergy by the state) and
of liberty of religious belief and worship. Milton was opposed to a state
established church as this sonnet shows.

ll.5–6. Perhaps a rather savage reference to the execution of Charles I.

l.6. Darwen stream: Cromwell had defeated the Scots in the Second Civil
War (see introduction to previous sonnet) at the battle of Preston. Cromwell's
capture of an important bridge over the River Darwen marked an important
stage in the battle.

ll.8–9. Dunbarr field . . . Worster: Cromwell's invasion of Scotland in 1650
was climaxed by his brilliant victory at Dunbar. By continuing his campaign
to the north he calculatedly left the way south into England open. Charles II

and his army marched south into the trap and were defeated at Worcester.
l.9. laureat wreath: given to victorious generals.
l.14. see John 10: 11–16. Milton nicely varies Christ's idea that the hireling shepherd will desert the sheep when the wolf comes by identifying his hirelings with the wolves.

53. TO SIR HENRY VANE THE YOUNGER
SONNET XVII

Henry Vane (1613–62) was an important figure in the politics of the 1640's and 50's. He took a leading part in drawing up the Solemn League and Covenant with the Scots in 1643 and was a member of the commission appointed to settle Scotland in 1652. He very successfully handled problems of administration and supply for Cromwell's Dunbar campaign and for the naval war against Holland (1652–4). Like Milton he was opposed to an established church and stood for religious toleration: this (as in the previous sonnet) is the point of Milton's appeal to him here. Because he disapproved of Cromwell's handling of these issues Vane retired from political life in 1653, so this sonnet is usually dated circ. 1652. Although he had taken no part in the King's trial he was executed in 1662.

ll.2–4. Referring to Roman successes that arose out of debates in the Senate and were hence triumphs of policy.
ll.2–4. The fierce Epeirot: Pyrrhus, king of Epirus, who invaded Italy (3rd century B.C.). Although victorious in battle he nevertheless sued for peace and in negotiation his chief minister described the Roman Senate as an 'assembly of kings'.
ll.2–4. the African bold: Hannibal whose successful invasion of Italy was successfully countered by the Senate's decision to adopt cautious military tactics in Italy but to carry the war into Hannibal's own country in Africa.
l.6. hollow states: perhaps a pun on Holland with whom England was at war: (i) hollow i.e. sunken land; (ii) insincere. This may give some extra force to *drift*: (i) scheming; (ii) motion of a ship.

54. ON THE LATE MASSACHER IN PIEDMONT
SONNET XVIII

The victims of the massacre were the Waldenses, a Protestant community living in Piedmont under the jurisdiction of the Duke of Savoy. The community, which went back to the 12th century, attempted to live according to the apostolic ideal of simplicity of worship and manners. They had suffered persecution before, but in 1655 they were ordered by the Duke to accept Catholicism or to leave their territory. When they resisted they were massacred. The sonnet is one of considerable power which gains its force by developing its theme in crescendo fashion.

*l.*4. i.e. before England became a Protestant country.

*l.*12. *the triple Tyrant:* i.e. the Pope whose tiara was encrusted with three crowns to symbolize his three-fold authority (to Milton a tyrannical claim) over Heaven, Earth and Hell.

*l.*13. *A hunder'd-fold:* cf. the parable of the sower in Luke 8: 5–8.

*l.*14. i.e. before it is too late.

*l.*14. *the Babylonian woe:* Babylon was the capital city of the Chaldean Empire where the Jews of the O.T. were held captive. It is thus in the Bible a symbol of tyranny and spiritual degradation (see Revelation 17 and 18).

54. SONNET XIX

Christ's parable of the talents (Matthew 25: 14–30) is concerned with the best way in which God can be served. Milton here meditates upon the active and passive ways of service. The talent which he has cannot be exercised because of the restriction of his blindness (*l.*7): the will but not the way is there. But this must not lead to any distrust in God's providence. The will itself is perhaps enough, or perhaps the suffering which his blindness imposes is itself a service (cf. 'Not blindness but the inability to endure blindness is a source of misery' (*Second Defence*)). A difficulty is that Milton does not say what the talent is: one assumes that it is his poetic and intellectual gifts. As things turned out he did not cease to use these because of his blindness though no doubt there were times when his difficulties must have seemed almost insuperable. Milton lost his sight early in the 1650's, and this sonnet is usually dated circ. 1652.

*l.*2: *ere half my days*: Milton can hardly mean 'before I am thirty-five years old' (i.e. half the normal life span of seventy years) as he was not blind then. It has been suggested that he means 'Before half of my working life is over' or that, given the fact that his own father lived to a great age, he is assuming that he himself has a life expectancy greater than the usual seventy years.

*l.*14. *waite:* possibly a pun: (i) serve as attendant at table, thus emphasizing his humble role; (ii) exercise patience and resignation (which is also a mode of service).

55. SONNET XX

A sonnet of grace and charm. Milton's Puritanism did not preclude enjoyment of the delights of wine and song, and this and the next sonnet reflect an Horatian epicureanism. This one particularly reflects Horace,

Odes I, ix and *Epodes* XIII on the pleasures to be enjoyed indoors in midwinter.

Edward Lawrence (1635?-57) was the son of Henry Lawrence, Lord President of the Council 1654-9. In his *Second Defence* Milton praised the father for his services to his country. This sonnet is usually dated circ. 1655.

*l.*2.   *dank:* wet.

*l.*6.   *Favonius:* the west wind.

*l.*6.   *re-inspire:* reanimate by its breath.

*l.*8.   see Matthew 6: 29. Christ cites the lily and rose as examples of beauty achieved without taking thought for the morrow. Milton wittily ignores that fact that Man is distinguished from the rest of creation precisely by his rationality and responsibility.

*l.*9.   *neat:* elegant and tasteful.

*l.*10.   *Attick:* Greek (Athens was the capital of Attica); hence simple and refined.

*l.*10.   *Tuscan:* Italian.

*l.*13.   *spare:* afford time to. Perhaps 'refrain from'.

55.   SONNET XXI

Cf. Horace *Odes* II, xi, for a similar epicurean unconcern about foreign affairs though Milton's close is more religious and ethical than Horace's. Cyriack Skinner (1627-1700) was a pupil of Milton's which may account for the rather severer tone of this sonnet. It is usually dated circ. 1655.

*ll.*1-4.   i.e. his grandfather Sir Edward Coke who had resisted attempted royal encroachments upon national liberties under the common law by James I and Charles I.

*l.*2.   *Themis:* goddess of justice.

*l.*7.   *Euclid . . . Archimedes:* mathematicians of ancient Greece and Syracuse.

*l.*8.   Sweden was involved in wars in Poland and the North 1655-60, and France in wars with Spain throughout the 1650's.

56.   SONNET XXII

See introductory note to Sonnets. This sonnet is usually dated circ. 1655.

*ll.*1-2.   Milton's blindness did not involve external damage to his eyes (cf. *Paradise Lost*, III, 25).

*ll.*10-11.   Milton makes the same point that his blindness was due to his exertions in political controversy in his prose writings.

*l.*12.   The audience for Milton's defences of the execution of Charles I was European, not merely English. His works on the subject were in Latin and his opponents lived abroad.

*l.*13.   *mask:* show. Milton has come a long way since *Comus*.

Both Milton's first wife, Mary Powell (d. 1652) and his second wife, Katherine Woodcock (d. 1658) died shortly after having given birth to children. It is difficult to determine about which wife this poem is written, though it is usually connected with his second wife and dated circa. 1658. The sonnet moves beautifully by a series of points of likeness and unlikeness between Milton's situation and that of Admetus. The latter was a Greek king whose wife Alcestis had laid down her life to save him. Hercules brought her back from the grave and restored her to her husband. Euripedes treated the subject in his drama *Alcestis*. Like Admetus Milton had his wife restored to him and rejoiced at it. But his wife is a *Saint* (because a Christian), and whereas Alcestis was touched by the pallor of death and brought back by force, Milton's wife appeared freely and purified by a Christian rite. Though both were veiled, nevertheless the spiritual virtues of his wife shone through her person, and Milton had the expectation of a second reunion with her in Heaven, a prospect which Admetus would not enjoy. It is worth nothing that this is the only poem of Milton's which closes on a note of loss rather than of reassurance.

l.3. *Jove's great son:* Hercules.

ll.5–6. A reference to the ceremony of the purification of women after child-birth (see Leviticus 12).

l.5. *as whom:* like one whom.

l.9. Milton makes the nice point that the spiritual attribute is now more real than the physical: *white . . . pure as her mind.*

l.10. *fancied:* i.e. of imagination. If this (and the veiled face) are a reference to his blindness, this might indicate that the poem is about his second wife whose face he had never seen since he was already blind when they were married.

---

57. THE FIFTH ODE OF HORACE. LIB I

An attempt to adopt classical metre into English. There were many efforts of this kind in the 16th century when there was real controversy as to whether classical metres and unrhymed verse could be adopted in English. By the 17th century the issue was little more than a literary exercise. So this poem is a craftsman's poem, but Milton hardly solves the problem of how to achieve Latin conciseness of effect in English. His syntax and word-order are somewhat confused. No certain date can be given to the poem.

l.5. *unwonted:* i.e. he is not used to such weather.

Really a sonnet with a tail (*sonnetto caudato*), a form used in Italian for satiric purposes. In this contemptuous mood (as often in his prose) Milton's mind moves with remarkable ingenuity of wit and punning. The poem is usually dated circ. 1646.

Title: The Long Parliament had abolished Episcopacy and had appointed the Westminster Assembly in 1643 to settle matters of religion in the state. Their new book of worship was accepted by Parliament in 1644, and the Presbyterian system of church government was established in 1645. For Milton's difficulties with the Parliament, see Sonnet XII, *l.*2 note.

*ll.*1–4. Objections to Episcopacy were to the power of the bishops (1), the forms of worship laid down in the Prayer Book (2), and the permitting of one person to hold two or more benefices concurrently (3).

*l.*2.   *stiff:* steadfast (even to stubbornness).

*l.*3.   *widdow'd whore:* i.e. the whore of Babylon (Revelation 17 and 18), the symbol of Popish and (to the Puritans) Episcopalian tyranny. The Bible does not say that she is a widow, but Milton may want to suggest that plurality (like a wife) may survive her husband's (Episcopacy's) death.

*ll.*5–6.   Christ set up the new covenant of grace to free Man from the old covenant of the law. The question of the relation of the 'free' Christian to the civil law was a very difficult one: Christ's saying: 'Render therefore unto Caesar the things which are Caesar's; and unto God the things that are God's' (Matthew 22: 21) put the issue without solving it.

*l.*7.   *classic:* the 'classis' was part of the system of Presbyterian church government and consisted of the elders or pastors of the churches in a district.

*ll.*8–12.   *A. S . . . Rutherford . . . Edwards:* Presbyterian divines.

*l.*14.   *packing:* plottings.

*l.*14.   *Trent:* i.e. the Council of Trent (1545–63) which had defined and established the doctrine and discipline of the Catholic church in the face of the Protestant threat.

*l.*17.   *Pylacteries:* small leather boxes containing four texts of Scripture and worn by Jews as a reminder of their obligation to keep the Law. Christ accused the Pharisees (Matthew 23: 5) of enlarging their pylacteries so as to advertise their observance of the law. Hence=hypocritical observances.

*l.*17.   *bauk:* miss, overlook. In 1637 William Prynn had been pilloried and had had his ears cut off as a punishment for his attacks on Episcopacy. Milton deliberately harks back to the time when the Presbyterians themselves were the victims of persecution. Milton may also be glancing at the fact that physical mutilation was a bar to the priesthood (Leviticus 21: 16–23).

*l.*20.   *Presbyter . . . Priest:* the two words are derived from the same linguistic root. The former merely has more letters (*writ large*).

ARCADES and LYCIDAS

As the headnote indicates, *Arcades* was written as part of an entertainment to honour the Countess of Derby. The Countess (1562–1637) was born Alice Spencer and in 1580 married Ferdinando Stanley who was created Earl of Derby in 1594 and died in mysterious circumstances (possibly through poisoning because of his refusal to involve himself in plots against the Queen) in the same year. By him she had three children: Anne, Francis, and Elizabeth. In 1600 she became the third wife of Sir Thomas Egerton (1540–1617). Egerton was a successful courtier (John Donne served as his secretary 1598–1602) and was created Baron Ellesmere in 1603 and Viscount Brackley in 1616. The earldom of Bridgewater was promised to him just before his death and was granted in 1617 to John (1579–1649), the second— but first surviving—son of his marriage to Elizabeth Ravenscroft (d. 1598). This son John had in 1601 married Francis (1583–1636), the Countess of Derby's second daughter, and it is his installation as President of Council of Wales that is celebrated in *Comus* (see introductory note to *Comus*). There is thus a link between the families for whom *Arcades* and *Comus* were written. The two families had enjoyed increasing prosperity and success under Elizabeth and the Stuarts. It was probably Henry Lawes who set the songs of *Arcades* to music, who introduced Milton to this milieu. See *Sonnet XIV*, introduction.

Arcades is a poem of graceful compliment and, as is appropriate for a work played in the grounds of Harefield House, the Countess's country residence in Middlesex, makes use of the tradition of elegant pastoral. It was written in the early 1630's.

Title: Arcades relates the setting at Harefield to Arcadia, the carefree pastoral country of classical poetry.

Headnote: Participation in entertainment by courtiers was also a feature of the masque (see introductory note to *Comus*).

l.2. What sudden blaze: the images of light and darkness in this piece are relevant to the occasion. It was played out of doors by night, and the Countess sat in the middle of a lighted space.

ll.8–13. Very much in the Jonson courtly tradition of witty compliment.

l.20. Latona: mother of Apollo and Diana who was the subject of Juno's cruel jealousy. Milton mentions her here as the type of illustrious faithful mother (cf. *Sonnet XII, ll.5–7* note).

l.21. towred Cybele: mother of Zeus and known as 'the great Mother' or 'Mother of the Gods'. She is described as *Towred* because she was represented with her head crowned with towers.

l.26. genius of the wood: cf. *Il Penseroso, l.154.*

l.27. i.e. they are of noble birth despite their pastoral costume.

l.30. Alpheus: Arcadian river whose god fell in love with the nymph Arethusa and pursued her until she was turned into a fountain by Diana. This fountain was on an island near Sicily, and it was supposed that the river Alpheus when it reached the sea passed by a secret channel (hence *secret sluse*) under the waters without becoming salty until it joined the waters from the fountain. Cf. *Lycidas, ll.85, 132.*

l.33. silver-buskin'd: with shining shoes, *buskin'd* here is poetical and conveys no suggestion of tragedy (contrast *Il Penseroso, l.102*).

l.36. yon princely shrine: i.e. Harefield House.

l.39. solemnity: feast.

ll.46–7. A very poetical elaboration.

l.51. harms of thwarting thunder blew: the damage done by thunderbolts which are sent by the gods to injure their victims on earth.

l.52. cross: baleful in its influence.

ll.62–73. To grace the occasion Milton presents a very beautiful pagan cosmology, based on the vision of life after death seen by the hero Er in Plato's *Republic*, X. In a region of intensely bright light Er sees the spindle of Necessity on which are whorls which represent the eight heavenly spheres. The spindle is turned upon the knees of Necessity. Upon each whorl is a siren, each singing a single note, the whole making up the harmony of the spheres. The sirens are accompanied in their singing by the three Fates who assist in turning the spindle. Plato's picture is a very imaginative one, representing a universe of law and harmony, and its audacity and beauty would appeal to an intellectual poet like Milton. He did not take the picture literally, but it provided the poetical and mythological tone in which the beauty and virtue of the Countess might appropriately be praised.

*l.*84.   *enamel'd:* beautified with various colours. A poetical word.

*l.*87.   *warbled:* melodiously sounded. *Warble* is a favourite poetical word of Milton's but it is used somewhat harshly here with *string*.

*l.*88.   *Star-proof:* i.e. so thick that starlight does not penetrate it.

*l.*97.   *Ladon:* river of Arcadia. Syrinx was changed into a reed by its banks. See *ll.*106–7 note.

*l.*98.   *Lycæus . . . Cyllene:* mountains in Arcadia.

*l.*98.   *hoar:* see *L'Allegro, l.*55.

*l.*100.   *Erymanth:* mountain and river in Arcadia.

*l.*102.   *Mænalus:* mountain in Arcadia sacred to Pan.

*ll.*106–7.   *Pan:* shepherd god of Arcadia. He loved the nymph and to escape his pursuit she was changed into a reed.

*l.*106.   *Mistress:* i.e. nymph that he loved.

62. LYCIDAS

Lycidas was first published in 1638 in a volume of memorial poems, *Justa Edvardo King naufrago,* written by his friends to commemorate Edward King, Fellow of Christ's College, Cambridge, who had been drowned when crossing the Irish Sea in the previous year. The poems in the volume are of different types: some (as befits poems from a learned community) are in Latin and Greek; the English poems are also varied though most of them are written in the fashionable metaphysical tradition. Milton's poem is signed simply JM. It is the most ambitious poem in the volume: none of the other poems can match the way in which it deploys its learning in mythology and argument. Written within the pastoral convention it is nevertheless unique. It is likely that this impressiveness is a very willed thing in the poem. Milton knew that his poem would be published alongside others, and it is reasonable to suppose that he wanted his contribution to be distinctive and memorable. When *Lycidas* was published in 1645 it was necessary for Milton to provide a headnote to explain the occasion of the poem. In one respect he had had a great stroke of luck. When he wrote his poem in 1637 his attack on the corrupt clergy had ended with the threat that they would in the afterlife be punished. But by 1645 that vengeance had been exacted in an earthly context since episcopacy had been abolished. It is natural therefore that Milton should with his sentence *And by occasion foretells the ruine of our corrupted Clergy then in their height*, draw attention to the way in which his vague threat had turned out to be a specific prophecy. It is interesting that Milton did not name King in the headnote. In that respect *Lycidas* is like *Sonnets IX* and *XIV* (though the *Trinity MS* text of the last refers it to Mrs Catherine Thomason), but unlike Milton's Latin elegy to Charles Diodati, *Epitaphium Damonis*, which carries a headnote identifying Damon as Diodati and giving some biographical information about him.

Milton, out of the stuff of pastoral poetry, has created a poem of authority and power. The structure of *Lycidas* is particularly noteworthy. The image of water is made to dominate the poem: Cambridge is represented by its river; St Peter is the 'Pilot of the *Galilean* lake'; Christ the one who walked the waves. Like Milton's other major poems it expands its occasion in space and time: we are aware of the vast sweeps of the Atlantic and of the weight of past and future in this event. It also moves by effective contrasts: the harshly satiric St Peter passage, the lyrical flower passage, the tragic vision of the drowned man in the sea, the serenely assured close, all making up a varied and dramatic pattern. The verse form also has a dramatic role. The poem uses metre and rhyme irregularly: the occasional short line of three feet and the rhymes occur in no set pattern. Though perhaps influenced by Italian poetry, this structure here helps to destroy that sense of formality that a regular scheme would give (it is worth noting that the metre does become regular in the hopeful close) and communicates instead the effect of unrehearsed grief.

But *Lycidas* does present an intellectual problem. Its disposition of Christian and classical material is baffling. The consolations towards which the poem argues are three-fold. The first is the reassurance that virtue is rewarded with fame in Heaven (*ll*.76–84). This is presented through purely pagan and classical means: the speaker of the words of comfort is Phoebus, and the judge of men's deeds is Jove. The concepts of the immortality of the just and virtuous, and of a sovereign and powerful God were common to Christian and pagan thinking, and it is interesting that Milton here offers them in their pagan form. But it should be noted too that Milton does not in this passage about fame say that the just are in Heaven but merely that the fame of their good deeds is in Heaven. Since pagan philosophy could be seen to allow of a blessed world for the just after death, Milton may have two reasons for his reservation. He may have in mind the point that this immortality was not, as it is in Christian Heaven, spent in the same place in which the immortal gods themselves dwell. More importantly he may not wish to say at this stage in his poem that Lycidas has achieved immortality since that would make his being in Heaven at the end of the poem altogether unsurprising and unclimactic. For it is clear that in the later stages of the poem Milton is engaged with showing the superiority of Christian over classical thinking. The pastoral world of *Lycidas* has no concept of God's providence by which the processes of the world can be seen as rational and ordered. To the pastoral world the death of Lycidas is a mystery for which there is no ultimate explanation. The nymphs and the Muse are powerless; the sea-gods are baffled. The pagan world is controlled by Fate (*ll.*100–103), or mischance and haplessness (*l.*164). It is against these confusions and bewilderments that the further consolations of the poem must be set. The second, that of St Peter, looks at the world in the light of the question of Christian pastorship. It will be noted that St Peter is not baffled by the death of Lycidas. To question that would be impossible for him since that would be to question God. His concern is rather to point out that God will not fail to provide retribution for the unrighteous pastors of his church, a concern relevant only to Christian thinking. And the poem's third consolation, that *Lycidas* is after all not dead in the spirit but redeemed and taken into the heavenly kingdom, is of course wholly Christian since the truth that Man was redeemed by his Creator's own human suffering and death is a uniquely Christian one. But we can now see the problem which Milton had in *Lycidas*. For if the speaker of the poem had access to this consolation all the time, why did he have to bother himself with Phoebus and Jove? It would be one thing to say that the pagan world got some things right, but it is altogether something else to speak in one part of the poem as though that pagan thinking is the only sort of which he is capable. We have the odd impression that the speaker is either playing some sort of inexplicable intellectual game, or else that he has been converted to Christianity at some stage in the poem. At one point of the poem it seems as though he worships in a temple, at another in a church. The Christian close is itself not free of the confusion: the concept of Lycidas being the 'Genius of the shore' (*l.*183) makes no Christian sort of sense at all.

One can see how Milton got entangled with his problem. He wanted to write an impressive memorial poem and to range his poem alongside the great classical masters of pastoral, and the classical mythology and allusions were a necessary part of that. But all that did not quite fit the case in hand. King's name was not Lycidas. King was a Christian, and Milton himself was passionately concerned about religious belief and church discipline. *Lycidas* is like the *Nativity Ode* in that it reflects, as others of Milton's shorter poems do not, the whole range of Milton's temperament and interests. But, unlike the *Nativity Ode*, from the purely logical point of view it solves its problems less satisfactorily.

The style of *Lycidas* is suitably varied. It has a poeticalness of manner that fits its pastoral mode, but it is also bitingly satiric and passionately exultant, all varying with the variety of the poem's themes. One interesting point might be noted. *Lycidas* contains a very large number of violently changed metaphors and paradoxes: Johnson was very right to call its diction 'harsh'.

Title: Lycidas is the name of a shepherd in Theocritus and Virgil.

Headnote: Monody: an ode sung by one of the actors in Greek tragedy. Milton is the first to use the word in the specific sense of a poem in which a mourner bewails someone's death. But his use of it may be influenced by his sense that he is in this poem adopting a dramatic role i.e. using a speaker with whom he himself is not fully to be identified.

unfortunately: through misfortune or mishap.

*ll.*1–7. Milton opens by stressing that he finds himself writing this poem unexpectedly (the berries he plucks are not ripe) since King had died unexpectedly. An elegy for him would have been easier to write if he had died in old age.

*ll.*1–2. *Laurels . . . Myrtles . . . Ivy:* all plants sacred to various gods, but Milton uses them here to emphasize the painful nature of his subject. All these plants are named in Virgil, *Eclogue VII*, and Horace, *Odes* I, xxv, 17–18 has the dark myrtle and green ivy growing together.

*l.*2. *sear:* a poetical word.

*l.*5. *Shatter:* scatter. Not as violent a word as it now seems.

*l.*5. *mellowing:* seemingly an error when used in association with *ivy* since as the latter is *never sere* the mellowing of the year does not affect it. Milton is thinking about King whose life was plucked before it was ripe.

*l.*6. *constraint . . . occasion:* as the introduction above points out the poem's argument opposes the Christian thesis of God's providence to the pagan theses of Fate and chance. This line in particular shows Milton's awareness of the pagan argument; *constraint* = force; *occasion* = an event that happens by chance.

*l.*6. *dear:* dire. Contrast *l.*173 where it means 'dear'.

l.13.   *welter:* roll with the sea. A poetical word.

l.15.   *Sisters of the sacred well:* i.e. the Muses (see *Il Penseroso*, *l*.45).

l.15.   *well:* fountain.

l.17.   *somewhat:* rather.

l.18.   *Hence:* away with!

l.18.   *coy:* modestly backward.

ll.19–22.   A poet's lament for a fellow poet (e.g. Moschus's lament for Bion, Spenser's for Sidney (*Astrophel*)), was a kind of poetry with which Milton, quite properly hopes that he himself will after his death be honoured.

ll.19–22.   *gentle:* courteous.

l.20.   *lucky:* propitious.

l.20.   *urn:* i.e. grave. A poetical usage. It cannot mean urn in the sense 'receptacle for the ashes of the dead' since Milton uses *shroud* in *l*.22.

l.25.   *Lawns:* glades. A poetical word.

l.26.   A very poetical phrase.

l.27.   *both together heard:* listened to each other's songs.

l.28.   i.e. at noon. *Gray-fly:* another name for the trumpet fly so Milton's conceit about its *horn* has some point. To call the horn itself and not the weather in which it is heard *sultry* is to increase the audacity of effect.

l.29.   *batt'ning:* feeding.

l.31.   towards the downward slope of the sky had directed its westward-bound circular motion.

l.33.   *Temper'd:* softened, assuaged.

l.33.   *Oaten:* the instrument was made of oaten straw as befits the pastoral mode of the poem (cf. Lat. *avena:* reed pipe, Virgil, *Eclogue I*, 2).

l.34.   *Satyrs . . . Fauns:* Greek and Roman demi-gods of the countryside who were half man, half goat (hence *rough . . . clov'n heel*).

l.36.   *Dammtas:* a character in Theocritus' and Virgil's pastorals.

l.40.   *gadding:* straggling.

ll.45–7.   The poetical elegy often saw the death of the particular individual who was being mourned as part of a process of general mutability and decay, and the lament for the transitoriness of Man's lot was a conventional part of it. It is interesting to note the absence of this from Milton. He remains concerned with the particular case, and it should be noticed how these other examples of disaster in nature (*Canker* etc.) are compared not to the process by which Lycidas also died, but simply to the way in which the news of his death affected the shepherd's ear.

l.47.   *wardrop:* stock of wearing apparel.

ll.50–7.   The nymphs mourn for Daphnis in Virgil's pastoral elegy (*Eclogue V*).

ll.53–4.   *Mona*, the isle of Anglesey, was regarded as the ancient seat of the *Druids*, and the stone monuments there were thought to be Druid burial places.

l.54.   *shaggy:* overgrown. Anglesey was called 'the shady isle' by the

Saxons, and Camden (*Britannia*, 'Anglesey') says that in ancient times the island was one vast wood.

l.55. Deva spreads her wizard stream: the Dee was regarded as a hallowed river, the haunt of magicians. Changes in its course were thought to prognosticate prosperity and adversity (cf. *At a Vacation Exercise, l.*98).

ll.58–63. Orpheus (see *L'Allegro, l.*145 note), a famous poet (hence *inchanting*) and the son of Calliope the Muse, scorned the Thracian women and was torn to pieces by them during one of their Bacchic orgies. His body was dismembered and his head thrown into the river *Hebrus* whence it floated down into the Aegean (*Lesbos* is an island in the Aegean). Milton had some difficulty with this passage and the *Trinity MS* versions of it are interesting (see text). The first version, by saying (of Calliope) that *the gods farre sighted bee*, seems to give more power to her than Milton gives to pagan figures elsewhere in the poem. His next revision allows no power to Calliope but by calling Orpheus's head *divine* seems to ascribe a lot to him. Furthermore, by saying that *heaven and hel* (might) *deplore* his death, this version puts the whole myth into what appears to be a Christian context. The final printed text clears up these two points. The different versions seem to show Milton's concern for the ideological issues of the poem and seem also to reflect something of the confusion of purpose in this respect that is found elsewhere in the poem (see introductory note above).

l.66. meditate the . . . Muse: i.e. sing, compose poetry (an imitation of Virgil, *Eclogue I,* 2: *Musam meditare*).

l.68. Amaryllis, a shepherdess (and object of love) in Theocritus' and Virgil's pastorals.

l.68. Neæra: a pastoral character of Milton's own providing.

*ll.*70–6. This continues the note of protest, arguing that the desire of fame is only the last of many infirmities of those who attempt to live virtuously. The argument is then refuted by Phoebus, *ll.*76–84.

l.70. clear: pure.

l.75. the blind Fury: Atropos, one of the three Fates (the Furies were properly the Eumenides, ministers of vengeance for the gods). She was often represented in a black veil (hence *blind*) with a pair of scissors (*shears*) in her hand with which she cut the thread of Man's life.

*ll.*76–84. See introductory note.

l.77. touch'd my trembling ears: in Virgil, *Eclogue VI.* 3–4 Phoebus plucks the poet by the ear. But Milton's statement that his ears were *trembling* makes the idea more violent. The touching is meant to convey reassurance.

l.80. broad rumour: widespread reputation.

l.82. all-judging Jove: the task of judging the dead in Greek mythology belongs not to Jove, but to Minos and Rhadamanthus. But Jove is a sovereign figure so Milton perhaps avoids unnecessary complication by making Jove himself the judge. The epithet *all-judging* is interesting since though it looks and sounds like those other compound epithets which are classically applied to Jove—'all-seeing', 'all-powerful', 'all-knowing'—it is not in fact found. Plato (e.g. in his *Republic* and *Georgias*) talks of the judgement of the dead though he does not say by whom they are judged.

l.85. *Arethuse:* see *Arcades, l.*31 note.

l.86. *Smooth-sliding Mincius:* river in Italy. Virgil's birthplace was on its banks. Cf. Virgil's own description of the river: 'where great Mincius wanders on in slow winding curves, fringing the bank with waving reeds' (*Georgics,* III, 14–15). By calling the river *vocal* Milton may be referring obliquely to the eloquence of its poet Virgil.

l.87. *higher mood:* showing Milton's awareness of the difference between the moral and pastoral elements in his poem. Virgil describes his *Eclogue IV* as one written in a 'loftier strain'.

l.89. *Herald of the Sea:* Triton, a powerful sea deity. He is called *Herald* because he is usually represented as blowing a shell and making Neptune's wishes known (cf. Ovid, *Metamorphoses,* I, 330–342).

l.91. *Fellon:* cruel, murderous.

l.93. *rugged:* a pun (i) rough (as winds); (ii) hairy (as wings).

l.94. *beaked:* pointed.

l. 96. *Hippotades:* Aeolus (son of Hippotes), god of the winds.

l.98. *The Air was calm:* the ship had foundered when it struck a rock.

l.99. *Panope:* one of the sea nymphs, often invoked by sailors in a storm. *Sleek* (smooth-skinned) is also an oblique reference to the calmness of the sea.

*ll.*100–2. See introductory note.

*l.*100. *fatal:* (i) doomed; (ii) resulting in death.

*l.*101. *th'eclipse:* eclipses were regarded as omens of evil.

*l.*101. *rigg'd:* made ready for sea.

*l.*103. *Camus:* i.e. the river Cam.

*l.*104. *Mantle hairy . . . Bonnet sedge:* perhaps attempts to represent the trees and grass lining the river. It has been suggested also that the *mantle hairy* is the academic gown of the university. *Bonnet:* man's cap. *sedge:* possibly adjective i.e. of sedge.

*l.*105. *Inwrought:* decorated, embroidered with. The word is a poetical creation of Milton's.

*l.*106. *sanguin flower:* the hyacinth. Apollo was so grieved at his accidental killing of Hyacinth (see *On the Death of a Fair Infant etc., ll.*22–8) that he changed his blood into the hyacinth flower (hence *sanguine*) (see Ovid, *Metamorphoses,* X, 169–219).

*l.*107. *pledge:* child.

*l.*109. St Peter, who was a fisherman on the Lake of Galilee when he was called by Christ (Matthew 4: 18–20). He was given the power of the keys (*ll.* 110–11) i.e. the power to grant or deny men entrance to the kingdom of Heaven (Matthew 16: 19). He is traditionally regarded as the founder and the first bishop of the Roman see (*l.*112).

*l.*110. *massy:* weighty (cf. *Il Penseroso, l.*158).

*l.*111. The metal of Peter's keys is not specified in the Bible, but the opposition of gold and iron was traditional enough.

*l.*111. *amain:* forcefully.

*l.*112. *stern:* angrily, in a manner that intended no reconcilement (see 130–131).

*l.*117. *shearers feast:* the harvest feast which should celebrate the end of labour and effort.

*ll.*123–5. Milton indulges in some very violent changes of metaphor in these lines.

*l.*123. *list:* choose (to grate their lean and flashy songs etc.).

*l.*123. *flashy:* splashing, frothy; hence insipid.

*l.*124. i.e. their pipes are very unlike the *Oaten Flute* of *l.*33.

*l.*124. *scrannel:* shrivelled, meagre. A forceful, possibly dialectical, word of which this is the first recorded written use.

*l.*128. *privy:* stealthy.

*l.*130. *two-handed engine:* a weapon that needs two hands to wield it and hence of great striking power; or possibly a two-edged weapon which can thus be wielded with two hands. In the Bible a two-edged sword is a weapon used by God to smite the unrighteous (Psalm 149: 6–7; Revelation 1: 16; 19: 11–21). John the Baptist sees Christ's coming as being like an axe that will hew down those trees that do not bear good fruit (Matthew 3: 10). That it is the weapon and not the person wielding it that is said to stand at the door is typical of the deliberately harsh incongruities of this poem, and especially of this section of it.

*l.*132. As in *l.*87, Milton shows himself aware of the different modes of this poem.

*l.*132. Alpheus: see *Arcades, l.*30 note.

*l.*133. *Sicilian Muse:* i.e. the Muse of pastoral poetry. Theocritus, the first pastoral poet, wrote about Sicilian life.

*l.*135. *Bells:* i.e. flowers (cf. bluebell etc.). A poetical usage.

*l.*136. *use:* frequent, reside.

*l.*138. *swart Star:* a deliberately paradoxical phrase. *Swart* means 'dark, swarthy' which is said oddly of a star. Milton seems to mean the Dog-star which was the brightest of the stars and whose influence when it rose with the sun was supposed to be harmful since it made the summer solstice the hottest time of the year (hence: 'dog-days'). Milton seems to call the star *swart* because its heat makes the complexion swarthy. But in these valleys all is well since here it looks *sparely* ('not amply').

*ll.*139–41. Another set of violently incongruous metaphors.

*l.*139. *quaint:* beautiful, usually applied to artificial things (i.e. 'skilfully made').

*l.*139. *enameld:* see *Arcades*, *l.*84 note.

*l.*140. *honied:* filled with honey-dew, referring to a sweet substance found on plants and thought to fall like dew.

*ll.*142–50. This passage seems to have been added later since it is written not within the body of the poem but on a separate page in the *Trinity MS.* By adding it, Milton increases the pastoral beauty of the poem and by so doing heightens the effectiveness of the contrast between this passage and the tragic realization of the horror of King's drowning that follows (*l.*154).

*l.*142. *rathe:* early ripening and hence dying forsaken (like Lycidas himself).

*l.*143. *tufted:* growing in a cluster. Cf. *L'Allegro*, *l.*78.

*l.*144. *freakt:* streaked.

*l.*149. *Amarantus:* an imaginary flower supposed never to fade (= Greek 'everlasting') so Milton is speaking very poetically and extravagantly.

*l.*150. *Daffadillies:* poetical for 'daffodils' (from Spenser and Drayton).

*l.*151. *Laureat:* covered with laurel (emblematic of his pre-eminence).

*l.*153. A very dramatic transition. *false surmise:* because Lycidas's body was not recovered from the sea.

*l.*158. *monstrous world:* the sea, the world of monsters (cf. Horace, *Odes* I, iii, 18).

*l.*159. *moist vows:* i.e. vows accompanied with tears. A very concentrated expression.

*l.*160. *Bellerus:* the ancient name for the Land's End promontory of Cornwall was Bellerium and from this Milton seems to have developed a mythological invention of his own about *the fable of Bellerus.*

*l.*161. *the great vision of the guarded Mount:* St Michael's Mount in Mounts Bay, Cornwall. It has a chapel dedicated to St Michael the archangel who was supposed to have appeared there. There is some wit in Milton's expression: the *vision* (i.e. the place where the archangel was supposedly seen) itself *looks.*

*l.*162. *Namancos and Bayona:* places on N.W. coast of Spain.

*l.*162. *hold:* fortress.

*l.*164. *Dolphins:* Arion the poet was robbed and thrown overboard from a ship in which he was sailing, but he was carried to safety by dolphins who had been attracted to the ship by the beauty of his singing. Cf. Virgil, *Eclogue VIII*, 'Let Tityrus be Orpheus,—an Orpheus in the woods, among the dolphins an Arion'.

*l.*164. *waft:* carry i.e. do not let his body sink into the deep.

*l.*167. *watry floar:* a paradox. A floor must be defined as a surface that provides support.

*ll.*168–71. Another passage with some violent changes of metaphor.

l.168.   *day-star:* the sun.

l.170.   *tricks:* trims.

l.170.   *Ore:* precious metal. Another violent change of metaphor.

l.172.   See Matthew 14: 22–33.

l.175.   *Nectar:* drink of the gods. Applied rather strangely to anointing oil. Cf. *Comus, l*.16 note.

l.176.   *unexpressive:* inexpressible.

l.181.   cf. Revelation 21: 4.

l.182.   *Genius:* see *Nativity Ode, l*.186 note.

l.184.   *recompense:* compensation for suffering and reward for virtue.

l.186.   *uncouth:* unknown. So Spenser is introduced by E.K. in the 'Epistle' prefacing *The Shepheardes Calender.*

l.189.   *Dorick:* rustic, unrefined (like the Doric dialect of Greece). Said of pastoral poetry.

l.189.   *lay:* a poetical word.

l.190.   *stretch't out:* i.e. in long shadows. Night is approaching.

l.192.   *twitch'd:* fastened tightly.

COMUS

Comus (as this masque has come to be called) was the second work which Milton produced in collaboration with Henry Lawes. The Earl of Bridgewater had been appointed Lord President of Wales in 1633 and his family joined him at Ludlow Castle in 1634. It was to celebrate this latter occasion that Milton and Lawes produced *Comus*. The masque was an important feature in court and aristocratic entertainment in the early 17th century. It was a combination of dancing, song, drama, and spectacle. It had developed out of a small entertainment consisting of dancing and a dumb-show performed by masked dancers into an art form much more extravagantly spectacular and dramatic. Its greatest exponents were Ben Jonson and Inigo Jones, the former providing the songs and the dramatic elements, the latter the stage machinery and decoration. Jonson's *Masque at Lord Haddington's Marriage* (1608) is a good example of the *genre*. The characters are mythological—Venus, the Graces, Cupid, Hymen, Vulcan etc.—the plot line is simple: Venus is looking for Cupid, and her discovery of him and then of Hymen brings to light the approaching marriage of Lord Haddington. There is music, singing, and dancing and some elaborate spectacle, representing the turning earth and the twelve signs of the zodiac, towards the end. The twelve masquers playing the twelve signs were twelve noblemen of the court. The masque is thus a cultured celebration of a marriage which the court world wished to acknowledge and compliment. This is the tradition within which *Comus* is written.

It is dominated by its occasion. Its point is to celebrate the reunion of the Earl and his family. Its setting is Ludlow Castle where the family have now moved. Its chief actors—the Lady and her two brothers—are the Earl's own children, his daughter the Lady Alice Egerton who was fifteen years old, and her two brothers, John Egerton (Viscount Brackley) and Thomas Egerton, who were eleven and nine years old. Lawes, who was the children's music tutor, had obviously briefed Milton very carefully about the nature and the opportunities of the occasion. Clearly circumstances did not permit of vastly extravagant spectacle and machinery, nor of a high degree of acting ability, nor of a lot of ambitious dancing. The resources that were available were the joyousness of the family occasion itself, the atmosphere of good will, and above all the poetic and intellectual resources of Milton himself. He had to produce an entertainment of pleasure and compliment, suitable parts for the children, and songs for Lawes. The Lady's effortless though clear-eyed innocence is a mode of compliment to the Lady Alice The brothers' concern for their sister, their eagerness to come to grips with Comus, are proper enough compliments to them. The children's teachers have also served them well: the Lady can sing; the Elder Brother can argue and seems to know his way about classical literature (*ll*.437–9). The Platonic and mythological elements also enable Milton to present the moral issue in a graceful decorative way. This moral issue is the triumph of virtue and the praise of temperance. It should be noticed how when the issue of moral testing comes to the fore the ideology of the poem becomes less extravagantly classical and more like what the characters themselves did actually believe. The two brothers do not mention Jove at all: they are concerned with Heaven (*ll*.416–18; 452–4; 599–600); the Lady's speeches too become more touched with a specific Christian tone (*ll*.213–19; 328–9); and the Attendant Spirit presents the children to their father with the same manner (*ll*.937–8; 969–70). At crucial points *Comus* naturally enough presses harder on the Christian relevance of what is happening. But it presses no harder than the occasion warrants. Its moral tone is not one of rigorous austerity. Milton's point is about temperance, and he is not arguing any especially esoteric doctrine of chastity. He is complimenting the Lady's virtue. Marriage is her own and her family's affair.

The whole tone is thus beautifully suited to the occasion. That *Comus* contains more explicit moralizing and more drama than other masques is explicable in that the resources available to other masques were on this occasion not available. Poetry is ultimately the means on which *Comus* has chiefly to rely. Like the other major poems in this volume its style is varied: chiefly pastoral and graceful (as fits the actual situation of the court in the country), it nevertheless also contains moral seriousness and some satiric sharpness. Since it is a dramatic work it contains rather more colloquialisms and occasional concentratedness of speech that belongs to the dramatic style. Like the other work it significantly expands its occasion: the Attendant Spirit's prologue sets the scene at Ludlow in a very spacious context.

There are two MS copies of *Comus*, Milton's own *Trinity MS* and the *Bridgewater MS*. It was first published by Henry Lawes in 1637. In an introductory dedicatory letter to Viscount Brackley, Lawes says: 'Although not openly acknowledg'd by the Author, yet it is a legitimate off-spring, so lovely, and so much desired, that the often Copying of it hath tir'd my Pen to give my severall friends satisfaction . . .' The 1645 edition, besides reprinting Lawes's letter, also includes a letter written to Milton himself by Sir Henry Wootton which also praises the poem: '. . . a dainty peece of entertainment . . . Wherin I should much commend the Tragical part, if the Lyrical did not ravish me with a certain Dorique delicacy in your Songs and Odes, wherunto I must plainly confess to have seen yet nothing parallel in our Language . . .' Neither of these letters was included in the 1673 edition.

S.D. The attendant Spirit: according to Plato (*Cratylus*) dæmons or spirits were the souls of just men which kept guard over the just on earth. Cf. *l.*42.

*ll.*2–3. Plato (in the *Phaedo*) argues that the souls of the just live in an upper earth which is to our earth as the surface of the sea is to the sea-floor. Cf. *Il Penseroso*, *l.*88 note.

*l.*6. The syntax is broken here. The subject of *strive* must be *men*.

*l.*7. *pester'd:* crowded.

*l.*7. *pin-fold:* a pound for confining stray cattle.

*l.*16. *Ambrosial:* heavenly; applied rather violently to *weeds* since ambrosia was the food and drink and anointing oil of the gods.

*ll.*18–23. See *At a Vacation Exercise*, *ll.*43–44 note. *High and nether Jove:* i.e. Jove and Pluto.

*l.*22. *inlay . . . the bosom:* a vivid conceit.

*l.*26. *Saphire:* blue, because they are sea-deities.

*l.*29. *blu-hair'd:* the other deities merely have blue crowns. Perhaps Milton intends to suggest that this makes Britain inherently of the sea.

*l.*31. *mickle:* great. A poetical archaism.

*l.*37. *perplex't:* involved, confusing.

*l.*38. *horror:* tossing (in wind).

*ll.*46–58. Another of Milton's invented genealogies.

*l.*48. Bacchus in his youth was kidnapped by some sailors whom he changed into dolphins.

*l.*48. *Tuscan . . . Tyrrhene:* the part of the Mediterranean off the coast of Etruria was called the Tuscan or Tyrrhene sea.

*l.*50. *Circe:* sorceress of the isle of Aeaca (off the Italian coast) who turned men into swine. Ulysses was protected against her spells by the herb moly (cf. *ll.*635–6). See *Odyssey*, X.

l.52. *upright shape:* this shape and his rationality was what was held to distinguish Man from the beasts.

l.58. *Comus:* god of revelry and nocturnal feasts.

l.60. *Celtic and Iberian fields:* i.e. France and Spain.

l.65. *orient:* shining (like an eastern pearl). A poetical word.

l.66. *of Phoebus:* i.e. caused by the midday sun.

l.67. Milton's allegory breaks down here. A person made thirsty by the midday sun drinks out of necessity not intemperance.

l.69. *express:* exactly resembling, in likeness or image.

l.71. *Ounce:* small cat-like beast e.g. the lynx.

l.73. *perfet:* fixed, total. Some paradox is also intended.

l.79. *adventrous:* perilous. Very unusual in this sense and possibly a usage of Milton's own.

l.80. *glancing star:* shooting star.

l.82. *Iris:* sea-nymph, who was identified with the rainbow.

l.82. *Wooff:* thread. A poetical usage.

ll.86–8. A compliment to the musicianship of Lawes in that his power is made like that of Orpheus. See *L'Allegro*, *l.*145 note.

l.88. *nor of less faith:* as faithful as he is knowledgeable.

l.92. *viewless:* invisible.

l.93. *fold:* shut up his sheep.

l.96. *allay:* temper (by cooling). A vivid conceit of the hot metal being cooled in the ocean.

l.97. *steep:* fast-flowing.

l.98. *slope:* i.e. shining with slanting rays since it has moved down from the meridian.

l.99. *dusky Pole:* darkening sky.

l.104. *Tipsie:* a very colloquial word.

l.105. *with rosie Twine:* i.e. with ivy and berries as befits devotees of Bacchus. Cf. *ll.*46, 55.

l.111. *of purer fire:* Comus is self-deceived. Fire was the essence of the spiritually pure and the angelic.

ll.113–14. Time is measured and regulated by the movements of the planets and stars.

l.114. *round:* a pun. *Round* is a dance, and the stars' movement is also circular.

l.115. *finny drove:* a poetical expression that occurs in Spenser, *Faerie Queene*, III, *VIII*, xxix.

l.116. *wavering Morrice:* the Morris was a grotesque, fantastic dance. *wavering:* reeling.

l.117. *Shelves:* sandbanks.

l.118. *pert . . . dapper:* spritely . . . little. Both probably colloquial words.

l.129. *Cotytto:* goddess of debauchery whose festivals were celebrated by night. It was a capital offence to reveal the secrets of her festivals (*l*.138). She was associated and sometimes identified with Proserpina, the queen of the underworld. Hence Milton's *Stygian* (the Styx was the river of the underworld) in *l*.132, and *Dragon* in *l*.131 since Proserpina's chariot was drawn by dragons (cf. *Il Penseroso*, *l*.59 note).

l.132. *spets:* spits. Vigorously said of the coming of darkness (and more especially of a womb, 131). The vigour is kept up with *blot* (*l*.133).

l.135. *Heccat:* i.e. Proserpina.

l.138. *scout:* a mean spy. A very colloquial usage. The reference is to the morning-star.

l.139. *nice:* over-fastidious.

l.139. *steep:* cliff.

l.140. *cabin'd:* narrow.

l.140. *peep:* a poetical, not (as now) jocular usage.

l.141. *discry:* announce, proclaim.

l.142. *Solemnity:* feast.

l.144. *fantastick:* see *L'Allegro*, *l*.34 note.

l.147. *shrouds:* shelters.

l.151. *trains:* scents laid to lure a wild beast into a trap.

l.154. *spungy:* absorbent (i.e. receptive to his spells).

l.155. *blear:* dim, misty in outline.

l.161. *glozing:* smooth-talking, flattering.

l.163. *easie-hearted:* credulous.

l.164. *hug him into snares:* caress into traps. A very successful conceit.

l.170. *My best guide now:* because it is too dark to see.

l.173. *unletter'd:* this is not an attack on country life in general which would be inappropriate in a pastoral at Ludlow. But Milton does not idealize that life any more than he idealizes court life (cf. *ll*.320–5). And anyway clownish rustics and bad shepherds were part of the pastoral tradition.

l.175. *Pan:* see *Arcades*, *ll*.106–7 note.

l.177. *swill'd:* drunken. A vigorous colloquial word.

l.178. *Wassailers:* revellers. This noun (from the verb) appears to be first used by Milton.

l.170. *blind:* totally dark.

ll.187–9. A very poetical conceit about the onset of twilight.

l.188. *Votarist:* devotee.

l.196. *dark Lantern:* a lantern fitted with a slide by which its light can be concealed. No doubt useful for thieves etc., hence *fellonious*, *l*.195.

l.202. *perfet:* very clear.

l.203. *single:* total.

l.207. *airy tongues:* voices in the air. A conceited expression.

*l.*211.   *siding:* supporting.

*l.*215.   *I see ye visibly:* possibly she does. The sudden bright appearance of the figure would make a very characteristic moment in a masque.

*ll.*216–17.   a traditional reason for God's allowing evil into the world which He had created.

*l.*218.   i.e. one such as the Attendant Spirit. Cf. *ll.*12–18 and note.

*l.*222.   Possibly another spectacular effect. Milton repeats the phrasing of the two previous lines as a point of art.

*l.*224.   *tufted:* adorned with clusters of trees. Cf. *L'Allegro, l.*78.

*l.*225.   *hallow:* shout in order to attract attention.

*l.*229.   *Echo:* a nymph who pined away with hopeless love for Narcissus until only her voice remained, hence *aery shell, l.*230 (see Ovid, *Metamorphoses,* III, 356–401).

*l.*231.   *Meander:* Phrygian river with a very winding course.

*l.*231.   *margent:* bank. A very poetical word.

*ll.*233–4: see *Il Penseroso, ll.*56–7 note.

*l.*240.   *Parly:* speech.

*l.*240.   *Daughter of the Sphear:* Echo was the daughter of the Air and the Earth. By *Sphear* Milton probably means the air which encircles the earth i.e. the heavens.

*ll.*241–2.   Translation to the skies, usually in the form of a star, was a mode of immortality common in mythology. Milton beautifully varies this by ascribing the same process to Echo in which case she will provide an additional (because echoing) beauty for the music of the spheres (see *Nativity Ode, l.*48 note).

*ll.*244–6.   *ravishment . . . raptures:* words which contain the key idea of being carried away out of one's self and describe (as often in Milton) the enchanting power of poetry.

*l.*246.   *vocal air:* air endowed with the power of speech, probably 'breath'. The breath (i.e. song) testifies to the holiness of the Lady's heart. The phrasing is very mannered and poetical.

*ll.*248–52.   A very poetical conceit about the effect of song.

*l.*249.   *empty-vaulted night:* i.e. the empty vault of night.

*l.*250.   *fall:* cadence.

*l.*250.   *doune:* hair.

*l.*250.   *Sirens:* see *At a Solemn Musick, l.*1 note.

*l.*253.   *Naiades:* nymphs who presided over rivers and springs.

*l.*255.   *Culling:* gathering. Milton is the first to use the word in connection with gathering flowers.

*ll.*256–8.   Milton is inventing his own mythological episodes. *Scylla* was a group of rocks and *Charybdis* a whirlpool, both of which perils Odysseus had to avoid (*Odyssey,* XII). Scylla was a nymph who was transformed (actually by Circe out of jealousy) into a pack of barking dogs below the waist: terrified at this change she threw herself into the sea where she was changed into a group of dangerous rocks. *Charybdis:* woman who for stealing the oxen of Hercules was changed into a whirlpool. *soft applause:* a deliberate paradox to show the effect of the song.

ll.259–63. This discrimination between the right and the wrong sorts of song reflects the literary awareness so characteristic of Milton.

l.261. home-felt: felt within the heart. The compound is Milton's own.

l.266. Diana was the lover of Pan as well as the goddess of chastity. Comus very characteristically stresses the former.

l.267. Sylvan: rural deity.

l.268. bleak: pale and cold.

ll.276–90. This dialogue, proceeding by one line question and answer (stichomythia) is imitated from Greek tragic drama.

l.278. neer-ushering: close-attending. Comus's word indicates his sense of the importance and social dignity of the Lady's person.

l.289. Hebe: see *L'Allegro, l.29* note.

l.292. swink't: wearied with toil. A poetical archaism.

l.292. hedger: a mean word that suits the occasion here.

ll.293–5. Characteristically Comus gives the brothers an occupation that is more appropriate to him than to them.

l.300. plighted: folded, billowy.

l.303. Gentle villagers: cf. the Lady's point about courtesy, *ll.320–5.*

l.308. Land-Pilot: deliberately paradoxical.

l.314. stray attendance: those who attend upon you and who have strayed. Comus's speech is mannered and conceited.

l.315. shroud: hide. Cf. *l.147.*

l.317. thatch't pallat: the lark's straw nest built on the ground. An elaborate periphrasis.

l.319. loyal: trustworthy. Comus is still using a language of politics and high station.

l.331. amber: yellow, hence light-giving. Cf. *L'Allegro, l.61.*

l.333. Chaos: ruler of shapeless and disordered matter.

l.335. influence: see *Nativity Ode, l.71* note. *damm'd up:* keeps up the idea of a 'flow'.

ll.338–9. Even if it is only the candle of a poor cottage made of clay not stone, and with straw not glass in its windows.

l.340. star of Arcady: Callisto, Arcadian princess, was changed into a bear by Juno. Jove (who was enamoured of her), in order to save her from hounds, transferred her to the sky as the Great Bear constellation.

l.341. Tyrian Cynosure: Little Bear. See *L'Allegro, l.80* note. According to

Ovid, *Fasti*, ll.107–8 the Phoenician (Tyrian) sailors steered by the Little Bear, and the Greeks by the Great Bear.

l.345.   *Lodge:* house in the forest for use of hunters.

l.352.   *boulster:* a long pillow. A vigorous expression.

l.357.   *heat:* any intense feeling. The word does not in the 17th century have a specific sexual sense.

l.359.   *cast:* forecast.

l.365.   *so to seek:* deficient (gerundial infinitive).

l.374.   *flat:* level.

l.377.   *plumes:* plucks out feathers that are moulting (*impair'd:* l.379).

l.378.   *resort:* crowd.

l.379.   *to ruffl'd:* extensively ruffled.

l.380.   *clear:* pure.

l.388.   *Senat house:* Milton chooses the most extreme contrast to ll.386–7. It is not perhaps the best example of security.

l.390.   *Maple dish:* a wooden article, as befits a man who has cut himself off from civilization.

l.392.   *Hesperian tree:* the Hesperides, the three daughters of Hesperus, were guardians of the golden apples which Juno had given to Jupiter as a wedding present. The garden where the tree stood was guarded by a sleepless (hence *uninchanted*) dragon.

l.406.   *unowned:* i.e. lonely. A conceited usage.

l.412.   *squint:* having a squint eye. A vivid figurative expression.

l.420.   *compleat:* perfect.

l.422.   *trace:* range over.

l.422.   *unharbour'd:* affording no shelter. A use unique to Milton.

l.423.   *infamous:* of ill repute.

l.425.   *mountaineer:* mountain dweller.

l.428.   *shag'd:* made rough.

l.429.   *unblench't:* unflinching.

l.430.   An important reservation. Milton does not intend the Lady to be prudish or rash.

l.432.   *moorish fen:* swampy low-lying ground.

l.433.   *Blew:* pale. A light was supposed to burn blue in the presence of the Devil.

l.433.   *meager:* thin.

l.433.   *stubborn:* reprobate. Or possibly 'fierce'.

l.433.   *unlaid:* unexorcised, and hence still able to walk and haunt.

l.434.   *curfeu time:* i.e. at the coming of night since they walk in the hours of darkness.

l.435.   *goblin:* mischievous demon.

l.435.   *swart:* dark (cf. *Lycidas*, l.138).

l.435.   *Faëry of the mine:* demons were supposed to haunt mines and underground workings. *Faery* here is not a friendly being. Cf. *Nativity Ode*, *ll*.235–6.

l.440.   *Dian:* goddess of hunting and chastity. She carried a bow not simply because she was a huntress but also in defence of her chastity. Milton improves the mythology for his purposes by supposing that the second use is the original one.

l.442.   *brinded:* tawny.

l.443.   *frivolous:* a pun. (i) trivial; (ii) having no weight: Milton is thinking of the metal—gold or lead—of which Cupid's arrows are made.

l.447.   *Minerva:* goddess of wisdom. In representation she was armed and carried a shield with the dying head of the *Gorgon* (*l*.446) Mudusa on it. The Gorgons were three hideous sisters who turned all that they looked at to stone.

l.448.   a vivid line. Her foes are not naturally stone, but are hardened as if by freezing (*congeal'd*) into stone.

l.449.   *rigid:* pun. (i) unyielding; (ii) that turn to stone.

l.450.   *dash't:* struck violently, destroyed. A vigorous word that makes a witty contrast with *grace.*

l.451.   *blank:* deprived of speech and act, helpless.

l.454.   *liveried:* i.e. to mark her state.

ll.458–74.   Plato's *Phaedo* was the source of this idea that virtue has the power to spiritualize, and vice to bestialize men.

l.464.   *lavish:* licentious.

l.466.   *clotted:* lumpish, i.e. it loses its spiritual nature.

l.467.   *Imbodies:* partakes of the nature of the body, i.e. becomes gross. A Miltonic use.

l.467.   *imbrutes:* partakes of the nature of brutes. A coinage of Milton's.

l.475.   *charming:* enchanting. Usually said of the power of song (cf. *ll*.243–63, 477), so Milton's application of it to philosophy is deliberately strong.

l.476.   *crabbed:* unpleasant. Not usually said of music so Milton keeps up his deliberate incongruity.

l.479.   *crude:* not capable of being digested.

l.483.   *night-founder'd:* an original and vivid compound.

l.490.   *iron stakes:* i.e. swords. Periphrastic.

l.493.   *Thyrsis:* a shepherd in Theocritus and Virgil.

l.494.   *hudling:* flowing swiftly and confusedly.

l.498.   *straggling weather:* straying ram (usually the leader of the flock).

l.500.   *next:* younger son i.e. next in time (not in degree of affection).

l.503.   *fleecy wealth:* poetical.

l.516.   *Chimera's:* the Chimera was a fire-breathing monster.

l.517.   *rifted:* cloven. The shades of the dead appear to Ulysses (*Odyssey* X and XI) from a rock set at a meeting of waters, and Aeneas visited the underworld through the Sybil's cave (*Aeneid* VI, 237).

*ll.*519–78. This sort of narration provided the opportunity for the poet to show his paces.

*l.*519. *navil:* centre.

*l.*528. *mintage:* impression stamped on a coin. Hence *unmoulding* and *Character'd:* engraved, imprinted (*l.*529).

*l.*530. *crofts:* usually enclosed land, but here possibly fields on the downs.

*l.*531. *brow:* form a brow to. A very original expression.

*l.*534. *Hecate:* see *l.*135 note.

*l.*535. *inmost:* most secluded.

*l.*538. *unweeting:* unheeding. A poetical archaism.

*l.*539. *then:* the time that.

*l.*540. *Herb:* grassy pasture.

*l.*541. *besprent:* besprinkled. A poetical archaism.

*l.*546. sing pastoral songs. A poetical phrase. Cf. *Lycidas, l.*66 note.

*l.*547. *close:* a word also applied to music=end of a musical passage.

*l.*551. *stop:* perhaps a pun: (i) ending; (ii) a musical stop i.e. aperture in an instrument. Hence in sense (i) a very *unusual* stop.

*l.*553. *litter:* curtained couch.

*l.*555. *steam:* fragrant vapour.

*ll.*556–9. An elaborate poetical conceit.

*l.*564. *harrow'd:* greatly moved.

*l.*567. *Lawns:* glades. A poetical word.

*l.*572. *prevent:* forestall.

*ll.*587–91. *erring men call Chance:* and which she would call Providence. The Lady will regard any encounter with evil as intended for the trial of her virtue.

*l.*590. *mischief:* worker of evil.

*l.*591. *prove:* evince.

*l.*594. *setl'd:* gathered together as a sediment.

*l.*597. *pillar'd firmament . . . earth's base:* poetical for 'heaven and earth'.

*l.*598. *stubble:* worthless rubbish.

*l.*602. *greisly:* grim. A poetical word.

*l.*603. *Acheron:* river of hell and of the dead.

*l.*604. *Harpies:* three winged monsters of grotesque appearance.

*l.*604. *Hydras:* many-headed monsters.

*l.*606. *purchase:* plunder.

*l.*607. *curls:* ringlets. Comus is suddenly and very effectively seen as a courtly gallant.

*l.*609. *yet:* nevertheless.

*l.*609. *Emprise:* enterprise. A word of chivalric associations.

*l.*616. *shifts:* stratagems.

*l.*619. *Of small regard to see to:* apparently of small reputation.

*l.*620. *vertuous:* endowed with great power.

l.621. *verdant:* a poetical word.

l.623. *tender:* soft.

l.625. *requital:* recompense.

l.625. *ope:* poetical.

l.625. *script:* small satchel.

l.626. *simples:* plants and herbs used for healing.

l.627. *vigorous faculties:* powerful properties.

l.629. *cull'd:* see *l.*255 note.

l.633. *like esteemd:* valued accordingly i.e. unesteemed.

l.633. *dull:* stupid.

l.634. *clouted:* patched. A rather low and 'pastoral' word.

l.634. *shoon:* a poetical archaism.

l.635. *Moly:* see *l.*50 note.

l.636. *wise:* Ulysses was noted for his sagacity and cunning.

l.637. *Hæmony:* Milton's own word and invention (from Greek 'skilful', or Greek 'blood-red').

l.639. *mildew blast:* blight caused by destructive fungi.

l.639. *damp:* vapour.

l.640. *furies:* see *Lycidas*, *l.*75 note.

l.640. *apparition:* supernatural appearing.

l.641. *reck'ning:* a pun made possible by *purs'd:* (i) heed; (ii) computation of an account.

l.645. *lime-twigs:* twigs were smeared with lime in order to catch birds. A vivid metaphor.

l.649. *hardihood:* boldness. The word is of Milton's making in order to create an air of chivalry (cf. also *dauntless*).

l.651. *lushious:* sweet and pleasant to taste and smell. A poetical word.

l.653. *high:* violent, angry.

l.660. *Daphne:* Daphne eluded the pursuit of *Apollo* when she was changed into a laurel (Ovid, *Metamorphoses*, I, 450).

l.664. *immanacl'd:* chained. The word is Milton's own (poetical) coinage. The Lady is taking up Comus's *chain'd* in his previous speech.

l.663. *rinde:* bark, here used very vividly for 'outward form'. The Lady is taking up the idea of Daphne's transformation into a tree from Comus's speech.

l.670. *April* and *primrose* are taken from their own nouns (*season* and *buds*) for poetical effect.

l.671. *cordial:* invigorating.

l.671. *Julep:* a sweetened drink of use for healing and comfort.

l.673. *Syrops:* sweet liquid used as a medicine.

l.674. *Nepenthes:* (=Greek: 'not grief'). Telemachus, son of Ulysses, on his journey in search of his father, was entertained by Menelaus and *Helen*

(daughter of *Jove*) at Sparta. Helen assuaged Telemachus's grief for his missing father by casting into his wine a drug, Nepenthe, which had been given to her by Polydana, the wife of Thone (an *Egyptian* physician) (see *Odyssey*, IV).

l.677. *cool:* refreshing.

l.680. *delicacy:* pleasure, voluptuousness.

l.693. *aspects:* faces. The Lady rightly selects the one element in Comus's rout that reflects their brutishness (see Stage Direction, *l.93*).

l.694. *oughly:* ugly.

l.697. *visor'd:* masked; *base:* low-born. She is referring to the shepherd's disguise which Comus had adopted.

l.699. *lickerish:* pleasant and tempting to the taste.

l.703. *delicious:* delightful.

l.706. *budge:* academic, since academics wore budge fur (a rough cheap fur of lamb's wool) on their gowns. Comus uses the word contemptuously for pompous, solemn teachers. As *l.807* shows, the pattern of instruction in Comus's own foundation is of a different order.

l.706. *Stoick:* the Stoical school of philosophy adopted an ethic of austerity and resigned self-denial. Comus's philosophy is Epicurean.

l.707. *Cynic Tub:* the Cynical school scorned wealth and pleasure. Diogenes, its most famous exponent, lived and slept in a tub to show his scorn of creature comforts.

l.715. *shops:* workshops. The word is not unpoetical or colloquial. The epithet *green* makes the phrase very vivid since the green of nature is in sharp opposition to shops which are of course the resort of artificers.

l.718. *hutch't:* stored as in a chest. The metaphor is made even more striking by its incongruous association with *loins*. Nature is both her own treasure house and a breeder of treasure.

l.720. *Pulse:* a plain diet of peas, beans etc.

l.721. *Freize:* coarse woollen cloth.

l.729. *cumber'd:* obstructively burdened.

ll.731–5. A very inventive and poetical exercise in science fiction: if we do not take diamonds out of the ground, then the monsters in the earth will grow used to their light and will thus no longer shun the light on the earth's surface.

l.732. *emblaze:* light up. A poetical word of Milton's own creation.

l.733. *bestud:* poetical diction.

l.736. *coy:* disdainful.

l.736. *cosen'd:* duped.

l.744. *brag:* boast. A very vigorous word.

l.747. *homely:* plain. Milton's lines point the derivation of the word.

l.749. *sorry:* mean.

l.749. *grain:* colour. A poetical word (cf. *Il Penseroso*, *l.33*).

l.750. *teise:* prepare for spinning.

*l.*751.   *vermeil-tinctur'd:* a very poetical compound.

*l.*758.   *pranckt:* dressed.

*l.*759.   *bolt:* utter hastily. Perhaps 'sift (like flour)'.

*ll.*763–6.   cf. Milton's arguments elsewhere that only the virtuous and the righteous had the right to political liberty.

*l.*763.   *cateres:* this feminine noun appears to be Milton's own invention.

*l.*769.   *lewdly-pamper'd Luxury:* that this is spoken by his daughter in a masque of this nature would ensure that the Earl of Bridgewater did not feel himself glanced at in this stricture.

*l.*784.   *mystery:* mystical religious truth.

*l.*790.   *fence:* swordsmanship. The metaphor was appropriate to the occasion since fencing was a courtly accomplishment.

*l.*802.   *dips:* totally suffuses.

*l.*804.   *Saturns crew:* i.e. the Titans who were overthrown by Jove and confined and tortured in the underworld (see *Il Penseroso*, *l.*23 note).

*l.*809.   In the old psychology the body was supposed to contain four humours which were associated with the four elements, and whose admixture governed the disposition. *Melancholy* was cold and dry (like earth). Hence Milton's figure of *lees* and *setlings.*

*ll.*815–16.   It was supposed that a charm could be removed by reversing the magic wand or by saying the spell backwards.

*l.*818.   *stony fetters:* a vivid conceit. Cf. *ll.*659–65.

*l.*821.   *Melibæus:* a shepherd in Virgil's *Eclogues.* Milton may intend Spenser by this since the story of Sabrina is found in the *Faerie Queene.* See *At a Vacation Exercise*, *l.*97 note.

*l.*826.   *Whilome:* archaic.

*l.*834.   *Nereus:* a sea-god. The nymphs carried Sabrina to the sea.

*l.*835.   *lank:* drooping. This is the only recorded use of *lank* with this meaning (usu.=flabby).

*ll.*836–9.   There is a lot of poetical diction in this passage.

*l.*837.   *lavers:* basins for washing.

*l.*837.   *Asphodil:* (from Greek: 'unfading'). A never-dying flower growing in Elysium.

*l.*844.   *Helping:* remedying.

*l.*844.   *urchin:* i.e. caused by a goblin. The urchin was originally the hedge-hog, and it was supposed that goblins etc. occasionally assumed its form.

*l.*844.   *blasts:* sudden blights; or malignant influences.

*l.*845.   *shrewd medling:* malignant, interfering.

*l.*846.   *viold:* kept in a small vessel. This participial adj. is of Milton's own creation.

*l.*857.   *adjuring:* exorcising. Peculiar to Milton in this sense (usu.=solemnly entreating).

168

l.862. amber-dropping hair: i.e. long golden tresses. A very poetical phrase. *Amber* is a yellow tree-gum and is used as an adjective by Milton to describe the colour of light (cf. *L'Allegro, l.*61) or of rivers of gold (*Paradise Lost*, III, *l.*358).

*ll.*866–83. In this impressive list of sea-deities Milton applies to them characteristics derived from his reading of classical literature.

*l.*867. *Oceanus:* god of the great ocean which was anciently supposed to encircle the earth. *Tethys (l.*869) was his wife.

*l.*870. *Nereus:* sea-god.

*l.*871. *Carpathian wisards hook:* the wizard is Proteus, a sea god who dwelt in the Carpathian sea. He was given the gift of prophecy by Neptune (cf. *Lycidas, l.*89 note). He also tended the flocks of Poseidon, hence his shepherd's hook.

*l.*872. *Triton:* sea god, generally represented as blowing a shell. He is half-man, half-fish; hence *scaly.*

*l.*873. *Glaucus:* another sea-god also given the gift of prophecy by Neptune. His oracles were supposed to be especially trustworthy. Hence *sooth-saying* is witty in his case: his prophesyings were true.

*ll.*874–5. *Leucothea:* (=Gk: 'white goddess'), sea goddess who had helped Ulysses when his raft was wrecked by lending him her veil which had the power to support him in the sea. On reaching land Ulysses threw her veil back into the sea and the goddess caught it in her hand (*Odyssey*, V). Her son Meliceste (whom she had saved from Juno's wrath by leaping with him in her arms into the sea) was also changed into a sea-god and was regarded as the protecting deity of harbours (*rules the strands*).

*l.*876. *Thetis:* sea goddess, daughter of Nereus. *tinsel-slipper'd* is Milton's poetical representation of her Homeric epithet 'silver-footed'.

*l.*877. *Sirens:* see *At a Solemn Musick, l.*1 note.

*l.*878. *Parthenope:* one of the Sirens who was herself drowned.

*l.*879. *Ligea:* one of the Nereides (sea nymphs).

*l.*883. *wily:* alert (not in bad sense).

*l.*890. *dank:* wet because rooted in damp ground (not in unpleasant sense).

*l.*892. *azurn:* Milton's own word from 'azur' (cf. *cedar'n, l.*989).

*l.*893. *Turkis:* turquoise.

*l.*912. *cure:* remedy.

*l.*920. *wait:* join retinue.

*l.*920. *Amphitrite:* goddess of the sea, daughter of Oceanus and Tethys.

*l.*923. *Anchises line:* the first British kings were supposedly of Trojan descent. Brutus, the Trojan founder of the kingdom, was the father of *Locrine.*

*l.*925. *petty:* small.

l.931. *molten:* flowing. A vivid word as applied to a river since it means 'made liquid by heat'.

ll.931–6. Milton's good wishes for the Severn are a somewhat poetical extravagance since the jewels and groves that he mentions are not found naturally near it.

l.955. *Stars grow high:* i.e. night is well advanced.

l.956. *the mid sky:* i.e. the middle of the sky.

l.958. *Sun-shine holiday:* cf. *L'Allegro*, *l.*78.

ll.959–64. In presenting the Earl's children the Attendant Spirit appropriately emphasizes the courtliness of their dancing which is without the less elegant *duck or nod* (*l.*959) of the country-dancers.

l.961. *guise:* style.

l.962. *Mercury:* inventor of music.

l.963. *mincing:* elegantly dancing. The word is somewhat oddly used since it usually indicates an over-niceness of manner.

l.963. *Dryades:* nymphs of the woods, though Milton here associates them with fields and leas.

l.969. *timely:* early.

ll.974–5. S.D. *the Spirit Epiloguizes:* speaks an epilogue. This and the prologue (*ll.*1–17) are imitated from Euripedean drama.

ll.980–2. see *l.*392 note.

l.983. *crisped:* curled, and hence used by Milton here with some poetical licence for 'wooded'. Cf. his use of *tufted* (*L'Allegro*, *l.*78).

l.984. *spruce:* lively.

l.985. *Graces:* three goddesses, daughters of Venus, regarded as the fountains of kindness and charity.

l.985. *Hours:* three sisters who presided over the order of nature and the seasons.

l.988. *musky:* fragrant.

l.989. *cedar'n:* composed of cedar trees. The word is of Milton's making.

l.989. *Nard . . . Cassia:* fragrant plants.

l.991. *Iris:* see *l.*83 note.

l.992. *blow:* bloom.

l.994. *purfl'd:* decoratively bordered.

ll.998–1010. *Adonis* was a youth, beloved by Venus, who was fond of hunting and who was killed by a wild boar. There are various stories as to what happened to him after his death. Spenser in *Faerie Queene*, III, *VI* describes the Gardens of Adonis which is the joyous paradise of reunited lovers (whose only enemy is Time) where Venus most often dwells when she is here on earth and where she enjoys the company of the revived Adonis. *Cupid* was the son of Venus who was in love with the maiden *Psyche*, but his mother and her sisters were jealous and encompassed her death. Cupid persuaded Jupiter to make her an immortal and thus they were eternally re-united. Spenser puts Cupid and Psyche among the lovers in his garden, and they have a child Pleasure. Milton readopts Spenser for his own purposes. His paradise is in the heavens not on earth. Furthermore, it has two levels, one that includes Venus and Adonis, and another *far above* (1002) where are Cupid and Psyche. Milton's account is also probably a revamping of Plato's paradise in the *Phaedo*. That also has two levels; the first, a purer earth for those who have lived virtuous lives on earth; the second, fairer still, for those who have purified themselves with philosophy. Milton takes this higher heaven over and fills it with details more suitable to his occasion. So his higher heaven sees the birth of two children (a point borrowed from Spenser), Joy and Mirth, which suit the Ludlow festivities and the Bridgewater children better than philosophy. But Milton still has to provide inhabitants for his lower heaven and for this he has recourse to Spenser's garden with Venus and Adonis.

*l.*1001. *th'Assyrian Queen:* Venus. So-called because she was identified with Astarte, the Syrian goddess (see *Nativity Ode*, *l.*200 note).

*l.*1001. *Sadly:* steadfastly.

*l.*1003. *advanc't:* raised up (to the heavenly sphere).

*l.*1011. *smoothly:* happily.

*l.*1014. a difficult line. Perhaps 'where the arch of light in the eastern sky gradually gets bigger'; i.e. as the dawn comes up.

*l.*1016. *corners of the moon:* points of the crescent moon.

*l.*1018. *free:* not subject to the power of anything else.

*l.*1022. *stoop:* descend from its height.

INDEX OF TITLES AND FIRST LINES
OF POEMS